AMERICAN EXCEPTIONALISM

A NATION IMPRISONED

IN

MYTHS

GHAZANFAR HASHMI

AUTHORSOURCE
MEDIA

American Exceptionalism: A Nation Imprisoned in Myths

Copyright ©2022 by Ghazanfar Hashmi

ISBN: 978-1-947939-93-6

Book design by Author Source Media.
Printed and published by Author Source Media, in The United States of America.
https://www.AuthorSourceMedia.com

AMERICAN EXCEPTIONALISM
A NATION IMPRISONED IN MYTHS

What is it that causes a country to be exceptional?

How have societies lost their exceptionalism in history, and how do you know when they get it back?

What are the benchmarks in trade, humanitarianism, military, economy, freedom, liberty, justice, and environmentalism that are required for a country to be great?

Has the recent chaotic exodus from Afghanistan affected the world's view of American Exceptionalism?

FOREWORD

When my friend, the renowned writer, scholar, and accomplished journalist Mr. Ghazanfar Hashmi, first approached me about writing the foreword for his book *American Exceptionalism: a Nation Imprisoned by Myths,* my thoughts first went to what may seem like an unlikely place.

When I was a young boy in Karachi, Pakistan, my older sister was a doctor working at a free ob-gyn clinic. Some days, my sister took me to work with her. I watched as women came in with their babies. My sister examined each baby before administering vaccines and medicines. Then, before they left, she gave each mother a big bag containing powdered milk, rice, juice, and other staples. On each of those bags were stamped the letters *USAID.*

One day, I asked my sister, "What does 'USAID' mean?"

"It means those bags come from America," she replied. "Americans give them to us so babies will be healthy when they grow up."

This was my first encounter with America, the beginning of a life long respect and admiration. Although I may have been too young to understand the word, any nation that cared for others struck me as exceptional. In many ways, it still does.

Many decades later I became an ambassador, serving as President George W. Bush's special envoy to the Organization of Islamic Cooperation. In the course of my discussions with the leadership of many of its 57 member nations, the notion of American Exceptionalism often came up, sometimes as a curiosity and other times as a hindrance. After all, nobody likes to be told *we're exceptional, you're not.*

While Mr. Hashmi is the real expert here, my diplomatic, entrepreneurial, and civil society experiences, as well as the comparative perspective inherent in being an immigrant, has given me ample opportunity to reflect upon American Exceptionalism.

I am skeptical whether any national exceptionalism can be said to have a tangible, concrete existence. Instead, it seems to belong to the realm of cultural and societal constructs. If "exceptionalism" ever had a concrete existence, it would surely require that exceptional prerogatives be balanced with exceptional obligations. The America that so faithfully delivered formula, vaccines, and medicines to Pakistani babies, the America that spent 5 percent of its GDP on the Marshall Plan to rebuild Europe ($13.3 billion at the time, over $1 trillion in today's dollars), *perhaps* that America was objectively exceptional. Either way, as I explore below, we are more than half a century on from that America.

I am not focusing only on the United States here. In "recent" history, other nations have claimed exceptionalism, whether the civilizing mission of Britain's empire, the universal liberty, equality, and fraternity of the French Republic, or the Soviet Union's alleged bastion of global proletarian revolution. None have weathered history's judgement especially well. There are other sources of claimed exceptionalism. For instance, Iran, Israel, and Saudi Arabia base their claims on being the physical and spiritual homelands of particular faith traditions. China and India point to their role as the cradle of great civilizations. These claims of exceptionalism, too, don't amount to much when measured against an objective yardstick.

As well, if I wanted to be provocative, I might posit that 1930s and 1940s-style fascism was merely national exceptionalism encoded into every aspect of state and society.

With my background, I am especially attuned to how national exceptionalism impacts foreign policy and national security. There is an inherent tension between belief in national exceptionalism and adroit diplomacy.

At a press conference in 2009, Barak Obama was asked whether he believed in American Exceptionalism. With members of the international press on hand, this seemingly abstract question created a tense moment, one with the potential for real consequences in maintaining constructive relationships with friends and allies.

As former ambassador, I consider Obama's response, "I believe in American Exceptionalism. Just as I suspect that the Brits believe in British exceptionalism and the Greeks believe in Greek exceptionalism," both insightful and a masterpiece of diplomatic threading-the-needle. I also consider it insightful that his response was promptly attacked from the right for being insufficiently patriotic. Editorials from the likes of Rudy Giuliani and Bobby Jindal suggested they would have been unsatisfied with any answer that wouldn't also leave America's allies feeling slighted or less than equal. Over the long run, that is not a good way to conduct foreign policy.

Modem claims to American Exceptionalism seem to jettison the notion of exceptional obligations and focus only on exceptional prerogatives. Today's loudest advocates for American Exceptionalism are frequently also advocates for cutting America's diplomatic and development budgets and skeptical of long term and codified commitments to other nations, even our closest allies.

That, I believe, reveals an important truth. American Exceptionalism has become a matter of domestic rather than foreign policy. It is one more tribal flag we wave for, or at, one another. This carries great risks. The very notion of exceptionalism has been used not just to explain away but to deny the validity of objective data or cross national comparisons. After all, what do such numbers matter if we are exceptional?

The belief in inherent American Exceptionalism has convinced large segments of the electorate that issues such as the cratering of American manufacturing, shockingly high numbers of children without health coverage, or the disaster of our early Covid-19 response don't matter. Or that we have nothing to learn from other nations in these areas. After all, "we are exceptional."

Prolonged engagements in Vietnam and Afghanistan did profound material and social damage to those nations, and we left them to clean up our mess. Beginning in the 1980s, we walked away from citizen-focused dialogue, reducing public discourse to a screaming match between the left and right. Internationally, we have given away manufacturing, given away innovation, and all we have left is the US dollar.

Because claims of national exceptionalism seem to act more upon emotion than reason, it can obscure things that actually are remarkable about a country. I would like to quickly note five aspects of America I find truly remarkable and commendable, and which I wish Americans would more aggressively protect.

America's open embrace of immigrants is not unique, but it is both uncommon and remarkable. And, in my experience, the extent to which America allows, even expects, immigrants to succeed is close to unique.

At the same moment Mogul Emperor Shah Jahan was building the Taj Mahal in India, America was building Harvard University. America's 400-year love affair with higher education has empowered our economy, our military, and our scientific and cultural preeminence. The extent to which America opens its universities and PhD programs to students from around the world is also close to unique. It is a decision that advances the whole world, not merely one nation. Over the long term, America's track record of wealth creation and prosperity creation has been unmatched, driven by capitalism and the private sector.

Fiscal policy is not as exciting as an aircraft carrier. Yet American's powerful grip on the global financial system, unprecedented in human history, is as close to truly exceptional as anything we will find. Because this aspect is underappreciated, we use it cavalierly. Every time we slap on sanctions—doing so is easier and less costly than other, potentially more effective options—we erode that advantage slightly.

I have saved the fifth aspect for last to end on a hopeful note. America's democracy, though it may be imperfect now and has been even more imperfect in the past, has endured for almost 250 years. In far shorter spans, many other democracies have drifted in and out of fascism, communism, and other forms of authoritarianism or illiberalism. Yet America has preserved against all challenges. I am hopeful that its present difficulties, including the dubious flirtation with American Exceptionalism in its current form, will prove no exception.

From my perspective, whatever it may have been in the past, American Exceptionalism in 2021 is a construct that obscures more than it illuminates, hindering much-needed public debate and an honest accounting of our strengths and weaknesses.

I invite you to settle in for an insightful ride as Mr. Hashmi guides you through the history, nature, and consequence of American Exceptionalism.

Sada Cumber
Former US Ambassador to OIC

ACKNOWLEDGEMENTS

To my loving parents, I send prayers of gratitude. I dedicate this book to them because without their love, I would have had nothing in life. They had not only been caring parents to me, but also mentors who guided my steps and enabled me to achieve my goals. They are truly the reason behind all the successes of my life!

To my family, wife and children, you are all priceless gifts, greater than anything I can imagine. If it were not for your help and support, I am not sure what I would do. I do not have the words to tell you how truly fortunate I feel to have you in my life. Thank you for supporting me.

A special thanks to Ambassador Sada Cumber for providing the intellectual feedback, encouragement, and becoming an instrument in getting this book published.

CONTENTS

AUTHOR'S NOTE

Knowing America while living within its borders is quite different from thinking about the country when you are living in other parts of the world. This experience turns out to be more unique and interesting when you live in a developing country, or where countrymen smell America's involvement behind every wrong.

Being Pakistani, I used to read a plethora of conspiracy theories and listen to talks and theories about America's secret role and policies towards Pakistan in particular, and the region in general. I have also spearheaded projects that were being run with the help of American aid and financial assistance in providing jobs to Pakistanis and contributing in a positive way to the economy of the country. It is also a historical fact that America has been providing military and economic aid to strengthen our defense, democracy, health, education, and civil society, meaning that America has been helping countries like Pakistan in different sectors.

At the same time, however, despite spending millions of dollars on the apparent well-being for the people in different countries, the common people, by and large, were not in favor of United States of America. They never praised the USA for its generosity and saw its role as suspicious. They believe that America, in the veil of aid, controls the economic, political, and foreign policies of the respective countries. They also believe that America is the Master, and countries of the third world are the Servant. There is a strong perception that appointments of key posts within the country are made in consultation with the political and military establishment of USA.

Why do Americans get a bad name and reputation, even after providing aid to so many countries and why they are not worried about this image? Why does America think of itself as a superpower? Why do Americans feel they are exceptional and unique, with a special role to play in the world? Why do they think of themselves as a chosen nation with a mission to spread liberty and democracy and protect human rights? Why do they regard themselves as born to lead the world, and the world should look towards America in every crisis?

If America is exceptional and unique, with a special mission to protect human rights, spread the ideals of goodness, democracy, and liberty, why do they support military dictators, martial law and influence the toppling of democratic regimes in other countries?

Does America possess the required traits and characteristics that make *any* nation exceptional? Is Exceptionalism only a myth or is it a reality? Is the rhetoric of Exceptionalism really needed for America to become a world leader? If America has lost Exceptionalism, what are the reasons, and what is its road to recovery? Has the American nation been imprisoned in the myth of Exceptionalism? Is Exceptionalism a hinderance in the way towards progress? Is American Exceptionalism a danger to the world?

These questions have been bothering and perplexing me in different phases of life, and I have made concerted efforts to find answers to these questions. I have been living in America for more than six years, and my insatiable curiosity has continued, which ultimately fulfilled my intellectual thirst in the form of this book, as my attempt to analyze the whole situation objectively.

The study of history is more than just dates of events that happened to others; it is a constant, ever-changing flow of ideas, lessons and rules that teach us about human nature. Some may even refer to history as the predictor of the future, as it recounts not only events but human nature itself. Likewise, a nation's exceptionalism is rooted in its history and glory, as well as its weight and influence on a global scale.

This book seeks to examine and explore domestic and international events that have been tightly linked to a nation's exceptionalism. A study of these events, and how they changed the world as we know it today, is a crucial undertaking for any nation. Leaders of a nation should learn from their history. As they say, history does not repeat itself, but it certainly rhymes.

Accordingly, this body of work is a roadmap for nations and leaders to control destiny by reviewing exceptionalism throughout the world. There have been countless examples in history of national exceptionalism that serve as a reminder regarding how history unfolds and how the future is formed.

INTRODUCTION TO EXCEPTIONALISM

For a nation, the term "exceptionalism" is not only a national identity trait, but also proof that a nation is unusual, remarkable, and truly phenomenal. In other words, the exceptionalism that a nation gains is linked with the idea that it is truly superior to other nations from all other eras. For example, we still regard the Chinese dynasties in the imperial era 221 BC – 1912 AD as exceptional, even though the most unexceptional and behind-the-times nation today would have had the upper hand. Exceptionalism is the perception that a species, country, body of institutions, movement and period is exceptional.

We deem America as exceptional because of its founding principles such as its natural law, liberty, limited government, individual rights, the checks and balances of government, popular sovereignty, the civilizing role of religion in society, and the crucial role of civil society and civil institutions in grounding and mediating its democracy and its freedom. The latter not only made America exceptional in 1776, it still makes America exceptional today.

American Exceptionalism is unique for a host of reasons. However, if the principles of exceptionalism are truly universal, and not tied to external factors, what makes American Exceptionalism different and unique from other nations such as Pakistan, Germany, or even countries with a different form of government such as China or North Korea. More importantly, can exceptionalism be diminished over time, and if lost, can it be regained?

Any nation can claim to be exceptional for any reason including the United States, Australia, France, Germany, Greece, India, Pakistan, Imperial Japan, Iran, Israel, North Korea, South Africa, Spain, Britain, the USSR, the European Union, and Thailand. Historians have added many other cases, including historic empires such as China, the Ottoman Empire, ancient Rome, and ancient India, along with a wide range of minor kingdoms in history. Just as ancient and past empires, countries and civilizations can fall, so too can a nation's rank and status of exceptionalism.

The United States of America is in a critical phase that will decide the fate of exceptionalism. Times are changing rapidly, and just like the United States has been the eminent pioneer of exceptionalism for centuries, today its exceptionalism calls for a change.

The future of the United States might appear as though it exists tomorrow, but it only takes a few glances at history to truly understand why and how American Exceptionalism can be understood by using the past. Looking at the past will guide us towards making the right decisions and avoid the ones that have plagued nations in the past and buried their exceptionalism forever. To do this, it is essential to look at how American Exceptionalism is radically different from other nations. This will serve as a reminder, a blueprint of sorts, for future glory for the case of American Exceptionalism.

ATTRIBUTES OF EXCEPTIONALISM

Throughout the world's millennia, a nation's exceptionalism has remained a mystery shrouded with the history of a nation and the national identity. This term "exceptionalism" has carried with it a lot of weight within and without each nation, which many leaders have used to lift their nations out of a rut, but what is the real implication of a nation's exceptionalism and to what extent can a nation be exceptional? What makes a nation exceptional for its culture, society, land, movement, and geopolitical importance?

A nation's exceptionalism has always had a problematic connotation as it was always difficult to define. It has been somewhat of an amorphous enigma; for a nation to be exceptional, it had to be especially exceptional and not just unique. Moreover, it had to be especially more exceptional to the point that other nations recognize how exceptional it is to them.

The attributes of exceptionalism are a myriad of fiscal, social, political, cultural, technological, theological, and ideological factors that make a nation exceptional. However, a question begins to evolve: "Is there a formula for a nation's exceptionalism and is that formula tightly linked to a nation's supremacy on the global international scale?" More importantly: "Can a nation gain its exceptionalism?" These are questions I have pondered in pursuit of understanding the blueprint for a nation's exceptionalism. In doing so, I have identified key traits and indices that prove to be the cornerstones of this discussion:

- Fiscal Policy and Economy
- Social and Judiciary Justice
- Constitutionalism
- Democracy
- Humanitarianism
- Health and Wellness Policies
- Environmental Policies
- Poverty and Homelessness
- Monetary and Banking System
- Trade Policies
- Technological Advancements
- National and International Defense
- Foreign Policy

In *People of Paradox* by Pulitzer Prize winner, Michael G Kammen states that, "A civilization without memory ceases to be civilized. A civilization without history ceases to have identity. Without identity there is no purpose; without purpose civilization will wither."[1]

I think the right step to take forward is to address the true core of exceptionalism that the US is undoubtedly blessed with. The healthy sentiment that Americans should have is to reignite that fire that was in

---

[1] Michael Kammen, 2012, People of Paradox: An Inquiry Concerning the Origins of American Civilization, Ist Edition, Cornell University Press, ISBN-10:0801497558

the hearts of every single American in 1776 that led to the stunning defeat of the British in October 1781, despite what all the naysayers propagated.

I think this book will rekindle that same fire in the hearts of all Americans today. I have heard that a lot of Americans are finished with the country, after the party of the left has taken over the presidency and the house. They are moving out, essentially giving up on their country. I have also heard Americans say that they refuse to let the conservative actions, thoughts and policies of the right ever have traction in the USA again. Notwithstanding, I am sure this book will help true Americans reconnect to their history and legacy.

PART ONE

A FOCUS ON WHAT MAKES
A COUNTRY SPECIAL AND AN EXCEPTIONAL

Exceptionalism alludes to comparison and hierarchy over other nations. Therefore, it is imperative to talk about the exceptionalism of other nations and how they became considered as a global superpower. There are many attributes that one can look to when considering a nation to be great, but every nation in every era has proved its exceptionalism in different ways. In this part, we are going to look at the exceptionalism from different views, what truly makes a nation great, and what examples have we seen so far.

CHAPTER 1

WHAT MAKES A NATION GREAT

It is imperative that we discuss what makes a country special and what it truly means to be exceptional in the pursuit of the underlying questions about American Exceptionalism. This question goes into how one can govern and make a country great. However, there is hardly any formula or plan that would lead a nation to be great. Instead, it's a collection of mindsets, goals, a system of government, and well-executed leadership. Nevertheless, we have seen many countries with great leaders, a good system of government, and a good vision for the future, yet they failed. Likewise, there have been countries with glorious geographical resources that have barely been able to scrape by in world economics, while other countries with hostile lands have become leaders of the new world.

Studying the history of both successful and unsuccessful nations gives us lessons we should never forget, and one of those lessons is that a great nation is built mainly on two things: people and their values. In the first section of this book, we will discuss exactly how some countries are greater than others, what makes a country great, and what makes them exceptional. There aren't many great nations that have made the world a better place, but one thing is for sure: America is one of the nations that has made the biggest impact throughout the world. Therefore, America is a good baseline, or point of comparison, to use when it comes to talking about the greatest nations in the world.

CHAPTER 2

THE METRICS FOR EXCEPTIONALISM

It becomes tricky to set metrics and standards for something like exceptionalism. Is it infant mortality rate? How much oil exists? The geography? The economy? The foreign policy? Democracy? Or is it something completely different? Does a country need to have certain qualifications to be admitted to the board of the top five exceptional nations?

To evaluate this, I have distinguished key traits and cornerstones for exceptionalism in hope of understanding the blueprint of greatness:

- Fiscal Policy and Economy
- Social and Judiciary Justice
- Constitutionalism
- Democracy
- Humanitarianism
- Health and Wellness Policies
- Environmental Policies
- Poverty and Homelessness
- Monetary and Banking System
- Trade Policies
- Technological Advancements

- National and International Defense
- Foreign Policy

These are areas where a country can be proficient, such as in health and wellness, economy, and political freedom. But what makes a country great is more than just "best country" rankings, data aggregations, or the Social Progress Index to shape policy. Overall, these metrics are used to describe how good a country is to its people. For instance, Norway is a great country as it offers so many benefits to its citizens, such as great education programs, excellent health care, social security, and a very low unemployment rate. Norwegians are also ranked first as the happiest people on earth, which is probably due to a combination of the nature of the country and governmental efforts. However, based on the above key traits and cornerstones, this does not mean Norway is the greatest country on earth.

Norway is definitely good to its people as it shows in their level of happiness, but that is because of many factors aligning, such as a good system of government, the abundance of resources, lack of external turmoil, and the unwillingness to venture out economically. But to call Norway a more exceptional country than the US because Norway has a higher happiness rate is simply inconsistent. The care and attention that *any* country gives to its people should be equal to the mindset of the people.

When it comes to what sets nations apart, there are two critical factors that must be met, and are what A. Linscheid theorized in 1943. He describes natural resources and the character of the people as the two greatest and most important pre-requisites for a great nation. However, the character of the people is the focal point. Palestine is not a rich country by any means. It is a flat land with barely any resources, but the character of the people is what made Palestine one of the greatest nations in history. The same goes for Athens, which was not especially exceptional in its resources, but today, ancient Athens has defined meaning with philosophy, drama, politics, and the study of human psychology, thanks to the values and character of its people. Conversely, the Democratic Republic of Congo is the richest country in the world regarding its natural resources, sitting at an untapped $24 trillion of minerals, metals, deposits of coal, uranium, gases, oils, diamonds and highly fertile land, while being one of the poorest nations. Other countries such as Russia are examples of why the land is not always the most important factor. Japan, South Korea, Switzerland, Singapore, and many more are known to have the driest natural resources, the most hostile land, volcanos, rough terrains, blizzards, and earthquakes, but they still managed to conquer those challenges and are now giants in terms of economic prowess.

At the end of his work, A. Linscheid talks about the constant struggle for a nation and its people to be great:

> A nation is what it is because of the character of its people, and character is not an inheritance but an achievement; not a bequest but a conquest. It is attained through the development of ideas, attitudes, habits, and skills.[2]

The sentiment for the mindset of people being more important than anything else is now even more prevalent in today's world. Virtual cities, imagined currencies and intangible development are reshaping what we think of as natural resources and their importance.

---

[2] Linscheid, A. (1943). *What makes a nation great? Peabody Journal of Education,* 21(2), 76–81. doi: 10.1080/01619564309535814

CHAPTER 3

WHAT MAKES A TRULY GREAT NATION?

"What defines a great nation is not only great guns,
or great wealth, but great magnanimity, great vision
and great compassion."

This is the sentiment of Mencius, a Chinese philosopher. This definition of what makes a nation great and exceptional goes according to what the US has done in terms of its exceptionalism. Lin Zexu (1785-1850) also expressed what it meant to be a great nation in the sense that it needs to be so great that it puts the interest of the entire world on its shoulders, instead of putting the fate of the nation on the world. A nation so great that other nations would sacrifice for its own well-being because if that nation is doing well, then it means that the rest of the nation's allies will likely do well.

Going back to Mencius (372—287 BCE): People are the most precious, society and nation are secondary, while the king is the least important among the three.[3]

---

[3] LC Ming, 2010, On Great Nations, Science Direct, Selected Papers of Beijing Forum 2005

This is certainly a rare sentiment that not many nations can claim to follow. Most nations have it backward with the head of state being the most important and the people being the least important. We've seen time and time again that nations who hold and apply the latter view end up, which is usually in either greedy corruption or bloody revolutions.

The path to a nation's exceptionalism is both tied to the relationship of the nation to other nations as well as the link of leadership. This is especially true in today's modern world. Nationalism might be the effort to preserve and strengthen the qualities of a nation, but it should not forget the rise of globalism. One of the defining moments of nations such as Japan was actually their meetings with the outside world. Japan had been a dormant nation reliant on old technologies and methods. It was its effort to meet with the outside world that eventually led to its rapid evolution in the 20th century.

For the longest time, it was hard to even define what a nation actually is. Only in modern history have people been introduced to nations; previously, they used to associate themselves with their tribe or family. *What is a Nation* is a book written by Ernest Renan. He describes what it truly means to be a nation in light of the national identity crisis that crippled Europe and other communities. He argues that a nation is a conglomerate of people that share a common endeavor and have derived a strong bond with an agreement such as a constitution to stay together and be governed by mutual consent (democracy) in the future. For example, this sentiment was felt by all French countrymen in their struggle to gain liberty, equality, and fraternity (Liberté, égalité, fraternité) during the French revolution, 1779-1789.

As Renan state in his book, nationhood cannot be complete without ties to the past:

A nation is a soul, a spiritual principle. Two things, which in truth are but one, constitute this soul or spiritual principle.

One lies in the past, one in the present. One is the possession in common of a rich legacy of memories; the other is present-day consent, the desire to live together, the will to perpetuate the value of the heritage that one has received in an undivided form.[4]

A strong example of a common struggle and a goal is the nation of Israel. The Israelites have struggled for centuries to secure a nation for Jewish people from all around the world. The holocaust was an event that every Jew throughout the world could identify with. The common goal was to build a secure nation. Nowadays, anyone who familiarizes themselves with Israelis knows they have a strong sense of nationalism.

> "To have common glories in the past and to have common will in the present; to have performed great deeds together, to wish to perform still more-these are the essential conditions for being a people."[5]
>
> – Earnest Renan

Renan also talks about an important factor in the creation of strong, healthy nations and that is to let go of hostility when it comes to race and language, and have mutual consent in staying together. The United States is a prime example of a country that has done this well, but there are many examples that show just how dangerous feelings of animosity can become when it comes to race and religion within a nation, as in the case of Myanmar and Iraq.

The sentiment that nations are more about a shared feeling of unity is the same concept described in the landmark study of

---

[4] Earnest Rennan,2018, What is a Nation, Columbia University Press, NY, E-ISBN:918-0-231-54714-7
[5] Ibid.

nationalism by Benedict Anderson, who views nationalism as a cultural construct with histories. Despite the imagined communities, this imaginary construct exists in the real world with defined features and borders. Nationalism took the place of giving people meaning after religion lost its political role.

THE CASE OF THE EU

In today's age of globalism, where there is an effort to eradicate such things as borders and national pride, the talk about what makes a great nation is even more pertinent. We have seen cases of nations that have defined their borders but loosely applied regulation to who comes in or comes out. The EU is a prime example. The European Union has some fuzzily defined edges that some may call progressive borders. While the borders of nations such as France, Belgium, and Germany are clearly defined, they are nowhere near as strictly supervised as borders between the US and Mexico or India and China. On the border between Belgium and the Netherlands, only a line exists that separates the two. Crossing the border is simply a walk to the other side. All European countries pay dues, they can vote on laws, and any citizen of one country in the EU is automatically a citizen of the EU which, in general, grants them benefits to go to other countries. Though this border theory is all fairies and rainbows on paper, it only took a few decades to show how this strategy is terrible for everyone.

To really understand the EU case, we must first go back to why the EU was created in the first place—to make peace with other nations. Europeans have been at each other's throats for centuries and this was impractical for both losers of war and winners. After the rubble of the Second World War, European nations had some thinking to do. In 1957, the EU was formed as a way to prevent future conflicts or war, but it was also a way to strengthen the relations between nations. There is no doubt this helped in the creation of some of the most advanced scientific achievements, as great minds easily came together under one shared goal. The EU really made itself a powerful entity, and people from all over the world wanted to travel and be there.

However, this all crumbled when some nations decided to do things a bit differently. Nations such as Germany agreed to bring in refugees from the war in the Middle East. The country is rich, prosperous, and thought that refugees would be good for the economy. It did not take much time for Germany to realize that this was a huge mistake. Germany had built a solid culture based on efficiency, intelligence, manufacturing, and creation, and the multicultural crisis hit hard as refugees from not only the Middle East war, but also from other nations in Africa took advantage and wanted in.

The EU is the opposite to American values in many ways. While the US values freedom, independence, smaller government, and individuality, the EU is basically one big government. The British have had enough of the bureaucrats, and they left. However, the immigrant crisis still stands today as one of the biggest failures.

CHAPTER 4

AN ASSESSMENT OF THE GREATEST COUNTRIES

Only a few nations have been considered as exceptional. However, each case of exceptionalism deals with different attributes that set them apart from other nations. Some nations are considered great because of their impressive rise in the global market, while other nations are considered great due to their long-standing heritage.

JAPAN
FROM AN AVERAGE STRUGGLING NATION TO A GLOBAL SUPERPOWER IN MERE DECADES

The leaders of Japan that conquered the Russian navy in 1905, such as Togo Heihachiro, were born into a land of sword-wielding farmers and feudal clans. The country at the time had no banks, factories, foreign relations, or even modern vehicles. The rise of the Japanese empire since 1865 is an example of how a nation can quickly scramble back to its feet to rival the leading nations in mere decades.

In 1866, Japan was a struggling country. Bandits overthrew lords, farmers could barely keep up, there was increased demand for products, a weakened economy, and growing tension made the political air thin. Japan was at the boiling point for revolution as the country was transforming. The civil war that followed in 1868 tore the old order to shreds, as rebels found themselves face to face with Gatling guns and western weapons. Proud samurais fought against the foreigner, but they were no match against modern warfare. As a result, a new imperial government was crowned victorious in 1869. The Japanese knew it was time for a change, but more importantly, they knew that it was in their favor to be flexible towards change, otherwise, the tides would be against them.

Japan first met the world when groups went to study in different countries to find out how things work. On paper, Japan was opposite to the west. While many in the US enjoyed outside events and loud parties, the Japanese preferred to isolate themselves in the beauty of their gardens. The Japanese quest for the outside world came with the realization of what they truly needed, and they came back home for true revolution. But this was not a revolution of one party against the other; this was a national revolution for the better.

Within little more than a decade, Japan showed the world why it is truly exceptional. It built railroads, established the rule of law among its people, built public schools, industrialized agriculture, banks, civil codes, telegraphs, police, prisons, postal service systems, hospitals, libraries, and even a constitution. As a result, Japan gained international respect and developed a strong army.

This radical change also reshaped the business and economy of Japan in unprecedented ways. Fast forward just ten years after the country had built modern toilets and started to eat meat for the first time, Japan became feared even by the British navy in 1897. Japan no longer needed the help of foreign merchants like Thomas Glover. They were now a true superpower that could engineer and make their own unique products even better than what they were instructed. In fact, even the British army needed the help of Japanese rifles in the first world war.

In fear of Japan becoming the target of China or Russia, the Japanese leaders sought out the best warfare players, the Germans. In just a decade, the Japanese had started to be less timid in their naval reach and started to engineer their own weaponry. By 1914, the student truly became the teacher. Japan had forged its way into becoming a unique modernity, while preserving and cherishing its culture.

Japanese exceptionalism was one of global discussion, as the country had climbed to the first world rank after it had made deals with the British in 1902. It would also defeat the Russian navy in 1905, showing the world why Japan was destined to be great. As a country, it does not have a lot of resources that would make it rich, nor did it have any international dealings until it was capable of venturing out into the world. Japan is an example of how leadership and the mindset of people is the true mark of exceptionalism.

BRITAIN
HOW A SMALL NATION ISLAND RULED THE WORLD

It's hardly possible to speak of exceptionalism without mentioning the largest empire in the world that would go on to become a nation where the sun does not set: Britain.

When the Vikings came to massacre the people of Wessex in 803 AD, the British knew two things, they can no longer rely on the protection of water, and they had to unite. For the longest time, Britain had thought that it was an impenetrable force that cannot be entered thanks to the surrounding water; however, the Vikings proved them wrong. The British saw what they feared before their eyes, an enemy that was better evolved. Eventually, Britain's weakness would become their strength. Their naval force had not only saved the British in the battle of Trafalgar and the Spanish wars but also expanded their territory and reach beyond the horizon.

The Renaissance (14th-17th century) was the age when Europe became exceptional, which was the precursor of European expansion into Asia, the American continent, and Africa, and the only way to get there was by sea. The British had already been through the naval struggle of investing in their ships and sea forces. As a result, Britain had become the leader in trade, exports, and colonialism. This had made Britain the number one dominator in the world with very few threats, except for France. Even after Britain's biggest loss to the thirteen colonies that would become America, Britain dusted the dirt off its shoulders and expanded into Canada, Australia, India, and other parts of Asia. The supremacy of the British navy and army allowed Britain to focus on trade, economics, literature, science, and philosophy, which is ultimately why the industrial revolution began in England.

Britain's influence on the world is one of the greatest, despite it losing its territories in 1997. Britain is undoubtedly an exceptional country that made history, thanks to the mindset and the common struggle of its people. Change and evolution are ultimately why Britain is remembered as a colossal power on the world scale with a legacy unchallenged. Today, no one can challenge the title of "Great Britain."

GERMANY
INDUSTRIAL LEADER

Germany's powerful legacy is often tainted by its predicament in the Second World War. The example of Germany shows just how important it is that nations ought to have the right leaders for the job.

Germany's history was peppered with achievements that changed the world as we know it after its defeat in the First World War. The history of Germany is the history of a people who have gone through a lot of hardship. Despite the fact that Germany was home some of the most controversial figures, such as Karl Marx and Adolf Hitler, as well as the recent turmoil surrounding multiculturalism within its borders, it still remains one of history's most exceptional countries.

At a time when the Germans were a mixture of different pagan tribes relying on agriculture, they had very little unity. However, what united them as a people were the Romans who wanted to conquer Germans.

Before the start of World War II, Germany nation had become an industry superstar, but the war led to its demise. After its defeat, Germany had to sign the Treaty of Versailles, in addition to paying crippling war reparations that stalled the economy. Inflation has never hit a country harder and there was growing tension.

The uncertain situation and growing desperation of German people provided socialists and fascists an opportunity to gain influence in Germany. They knew that Germans were not happy about the war and wanted things to get better, so the Nazi party fueled that anger and frustration into something tangible. The conservatives thought they could contain and control Hitler, but he was too powerful and his influence only grew stronger. After he came into power, it snowballed into him becoming the center of the Second World War. It's safe to say that Nazism plagued Germany and its history. Some even called for the abolition of Germany altogether after the Second World War.

All these examples show that to be an exceptional nation, the country does not have to have the best resources or wealth. Instead, it's more important to have a nation that is devoted to a shared goal and shared values.

In the case of Japan, though the nation was torn apart due to foreigners and globalization, the people of Japan had a common goal which was to be up to standards of the first world rank.

Germany was a compilation of tribes that had different gods, different cultures, and languages, and they even defined their nationality differently. However, the people were united by the threat of the Romans. Though Germany still struggles today with its identity, no one can deny its manufacturing and industrial power.

The name United Kingdom fits the country because it describes its struggles with invaders and its reach to conquer a quarter of the entire world.

CHAPTER 5

THE STANDARDS
OF EXCEPTIONAL COUNTRIES

Examples around the world of exceptional and unique countries show there are a few elements that can make a country special and exceptional. Of course, the rules set by Ernest Renan concerning unity and harmony within a nation for a common goal must remain true. Here are standards that can be agreed upon when it comes to great nations:

Democracy: Voting in fair elections is the bedrock of democracy. Every vote is equal, and every citizen is equally responsible for their own vote.

Checks and Balances: Throughout American history—and in countless other countries—we have seen time and again how dangerous it is to give one party the full power. The constitution of the United States is one that learned from the mistakes of the past and perfectly crafted a system where any branch of the government be it the legislative, executive, or judicial cannot be tyrannical. In other nations, one party eventually gets tyrannical as it gains too much power, be it the church, the king, the military, or the government.

Transparency: Trust is the most important element when it comes to creating unity. All parties must trust their government or those in positions of power. This can be access to data, consistency with applying the full extent of the law to each and every single citizen, or by being vocal when it comes to planning.

Investment in people: One of the most important factors in the success of a nation is investing in the future. This primarily means investing in educating its people, which will lead to equal opportunity for financial success. It's also about investing in the health of its citizens.

Clearly defined borders: A nation that does not have strong borders cannot guarantee equality for its people. Borders not only offer security from outside threats, they also offer equality of opportunity, protection of the land, water, and the national soil.

Economic growth: Ensuring a constant growth of a nation's economy is the number one way to help the nation become successful. Economies need strong employees and citizens.

Social and judiciary justice: Courts exist in order to guarantee liberty, improve social order, resolve disputes, maintain the rule of law, provide equal protection, and to guarantee due process of law.

Technological advancements: A lesson to be remembered is that evolution is just as important as preserving the laws and constitution of a nation. The world is moving at an unparalleled pace and this is especially true of the technological sector. Every nation must invest in its technological and manufacturing system in order to ensure that it never falls behind.

Foreign policy: All states coexist in the international system; this is a fact and to try to fight is futile. Even countries such as North Korea that display a strong rejection towards the outside world have started to adopt a foreign policy. Not to mention, foreign policy is important for building and maintaining strong ally relations. For example, Japan did not become a leading nation by separating itself from the world. Only when the country opened its doors to the outside world did Japan become a superpower and established strong trade with other nations.

Wealth: A nation must find ways to allocate funds for the prosperity of its people and for long term growth. Some nations have obvious ways to find wealth such as natural resources; however, the existence of a natural resource itself is not a predictor of a nation's success.

The United States, China, and Russia have been among the most prosperous nations and they are also nations that have huge amounts of natural resources such as gas, oils, minerals, metals, and uranium. Some nations can find ways to be wealthier outside of their natural resources such as Japan, Honk Kong, and Taiwan.

The trend that history teaches us is that a nation's land is extremely important. No successful nation has led the world from the Sahara Desert or the freezing cold of the poles.

CHAPTER 6

THE WEALTH AND
EXCEPTIONALISM OF NATIONS

There is no doubt today that exceptional nations are wealthy. Wealth is important in many factors, including progress, protection and making sure that every citizen is provided for.

China is an exceptional country largely because of its economical prowess over the world, and it is likely to stay exceptional globally because of the plans that it has for the future. The US is also as wealthy in many ways. The US is around 5 percent of the world's population, but it produces nearly a quarter of the world's GDP. The economy of the US is in a decline, but that does not mean the US is doing bad overall. Historically, the US has always been right where it needs to be in order to grow and reign supreme. Despite the loss of jobs, the country still holds the mantle for the world's most effective entrepreneurial nation that makes new technologies. The US has been on top of the industrial age and now it is on top of the information age.

Wealth is also that of ideas, and nations that are exceptional are no strangers to helping science and technology. The United States has produced 75 million cited scientific pieces of research in just 12 years starting from 1996. UK was second with 18 million and other exceptional nations such as Japan, Germany, and France have followed.

The discussion of scientific research is very important when it comes to wealth because it can be a unit to measure our understanding of the world and what the future may hold. Thanks to the United States' advancements in science, the green revolution happened to quell the fear of starvation in many countries due to high yield disease resistant crops. Billions are now alive because of this American achievement as America took on humanity's calamity—famine. Yuval Noah Harari described the three calamities in his book *Homo Deus* as war, disease, and famine, and America has addressed all three. The green revolution as a scientific achievement in the world of agriculture is highly underrated. Though this is not going to stop famine throughout the world, populations are now facing a bigger risk of dying from overeating than from famine.

PART TWO

THE CASE OF AMERICAN EXCEPTIONALISM: THE LEGACY

INTRODUCTION

No discussion of exceptionalism can be complete without discussing about the best case of all, the United States of America. After talking about what makes certain countries great, it is only fitting to examine the case of the United States as a nation that has truly earned the respect of other nations and became the leader of the free world at a certain point.

American Exceptionalism is a great story and it is what this part of the book will discuss. First, we will talk about the case for American Exceptionalism. We will dive into some history of how this phrase came to be word for word, and we will discuss how this sentiment began in the spirit of Americans. The rise, fall, and rebirth of this phrase is an interesting phenomenon that reflects the feelings of Americans. A discussion about American values is also included, as well as constitutionalism, republicanism, and the American Creed.

CHAPTER 1

THE CASE FOR AMERICAN EXCEPTIONALISM

The conception of the United States is unique and revolutionary. When America was shaping its path to become the leader of various world sectors, many argued that it's more or less ahead of its time. The reason is because, as a nation, the US has achieved what civilizations have not been able to do in the matter of a few decades because of the cumulative effort of every American. Even the term "American" connotes something different than nationalism; it has a sense of exceptionalism.

Seymour Martin Lipset, a political scientist writes in his book, *American Exceptionalism, A Double-Edged Sword*, "Being an American, however, is an ideological commitment. It is not a matter of birth. Those who reject American values are un-American"[6] He referred to G. K. Chesterton, who believed in American Exceptionalism and quoted his remarks:

America is the only nation in the world that is founded on a creed. That creed is set forth with dogmatic and even theological lucidity in the Declaration of Independence ...[7]

---

[6] Lipset, Seamour Martin,1997, American Exceptionalism: A Double-Edged sword, The American historical Review, Vol.102 No.3 (June 1997) Oxford University Press
[7] Stephen M. Walt, The Myth of American Exceptionalism, Foreign Policy, November 2011.

As noted in the Introduction, the nation's ideology can be described in five words: liberty, egalitarianism, individualism, populism, and laissez-faire, and these sentiments have been shared by every American including founding fathers and the recent generation. However, a country with these ideals is truly revolutionary, and most countries with some type of exceptionalism display a certain loyalty, a submission, a selflessness to the king, country, or theology. In the American Creed, this is different, everyone values liberty, egalitarianism, individualism, populism, and laissez-faire without being subject to a king, a priest, a shaman, or a prophet, and everyone is free in their actions and thoughts. While we might regard this line of thinking as natural and casual, this is only thanks to the modern age.

In previous generations, anyone who spouts such nonsense about liberty, egalitarianism, individualism, populism, and laissez-faire is a heretic, a fool, and probably an anarchist. This is what made the US truly exceptional: the individual became the center of the nation and not the periphery. Despite all that, Americans show a unique sense of nationalism that transcends all conventional forms. In other words, the very fact that the United States values the individual and their freedom is what made Americans love America. This goes for everything that makes America great—its foundation, culture, history, constitution, values, and individualism. The latter is what made Alexander Hamilton believe that Americans would earn the admiration of all mankind.

Over the last two centuries, prominent Americans have described the United States as an "empire of liberty," a "shining city on a hill," the "last best hope of Earth," the "leader of the free world," and the "indispensable nation." These enduring tropes explain why all presidential candidates feel compelled to offer ritualistic paeans to America's greatness and why Barack Obama landed in hot water—most recently, from Mitt Romney—for saying that, while he believed in American Exceptionalism, it was no different from British exceptionalism, Greek exceptionalism, or any other country's brand of patriotic chest-thumping. To the contrary, most statements of

American Exceptionalism presume that America's values, political system, and history are unique and worthy of universal admiration. They also imply that the United States is both destined and entitled to play a distinct and positive role on the world stage.

Democracy in America by Alexis de Tocqueville is regarded as cannon when it comes to understanding why America was great. The book describes how America was the pioneer and the leading example of all nations to follow when it comes to freedom and unity. Moreover, the book played a central role in influencing the politicians, philosophers, and historians to understand this concept and dominated the discourse of Exceptionalism.

However, he warned that as individualistic as the United States seems, it might commit a crime against individuality itself. The United States is certainly democratic, but it lacks the individual and personal influence of every American, which can cause what is known as "tyranny of the majority." Tocqueville's statement on the side effect of tyranny of the majority in 1835 was seen as laughable in the sense that America would never face such a problem. Yet, a reader of this work in contemporary times will see it as nothing short of a prophecy. As the editors of History.com note, "Tocqueville believed that equality was the great political and social idea of his era, and he thought that the United States offered the most advanced example of equality in action."[8]

The sentiment that America is great has been shared by many people of different eras and President Reagan called the country a "Shining City on a Hill … I've always believed that this blessed land was set apart in a special way."[9]

Other contemporary writers, such as Deborah Madsen, author of the book called *American Exceptionalism*, note that American Exceptionalism has always faced counter exceptionalism ideologies by Native

---

[8] Tocqueville, Alexis de, *Democracy in America*, Updated: June 7, 2019 Original Nov 9, 2009, History.com Editors.
[9] David Frum, 2021, Is America Still the 'Shining City on a Hill'?, The Atlantic.

American, Chinese, African American, and Asian writers. Mason states, "Exceptionalism was the legacy of the Old World for the New, but exceptionalism is now the legacy of the United States for us all."[10]

Going back to the Puritan settlers who arrived in North America, and who viewed America as the Promised Land, Perry Miller, an American intellectual historian and a co-founder of the field of American Studies, views these encounters as a brief recognition into the wilderness. This view was held by Puritans who viewed America as the land they would prosper in thanks to God, but it has also been viewed as the best hope of earth according to presidents like Lincoln and Kennedy.

---

[10] Debora L. Madsen, 1998, *American Exceptionalism*, (pp 166) Jackson: University Press of Mississippi.

CHAPTER 2

ORIGIN AND HISTORY OF THE PHRASE

American Exceptionalism will either trigger feelings of anti-Americanism or resonate within the hearts of patriots. The reaction people have to hear about their nation's exceptionalism usually results with either questioning the validity of the statement or engaging in nostalgia throwbacks about "the good old days." Until around 2010, very few people actually talked about or heard the term American Exceptionalism. The term gained popularity as a short, punchy slogan that could be used for both opposition parties, when John McCain attacked Barack Obama concerning his disbelief in the idea that America was exceptional.

American Exceptionalism is not merely saying the United States is different from other nations in its uniqueness. Rather, it hints at a belief that the United States is a country that follows a much different path historically. In addition, the United States is not just a country that is bigger, more opportunistic, and wealthier, it's a country that has been purposed to be the exceptional.

The term "Exceptionalism" was first used to describe the innovative social element that America was blessed with in de Tocqueville's book, *Democracy in America*. He believed that America offered the best example of equality in action of governing. The Republic and the rule of the individual was truly exceptional at the time when monarchs and dictators were the norm. America was criticized, since no one believed that a group of people could decide the fate of their country. However, this would be the first of several examples of American Exceptionalism, as the model of the Republic and individualism proved to be best.

Scholars such as Greene, 1993, argue that the idea of American Exceptionalism dates back to when settlers from Britain came to America and established the colonies. However, Miller believes that this idea started around the time that puritans came into the New World, and looking at it as the new Garden of Eden. This stems from the idea that American Exceptionalism started with the notion that America was the godly promised land for Puritans.

John Winthrop, English lawyer, and famous thinker of his era, led the ship named *Arabella* towards the new world with the puritans that escaped religious persecution from England. At that time, puritans had different beliefs, which was frowned upon by the present-day mores. John Winthrop and his fleet of around 1,000 puritans finally arrived on the shores of the New World in 1630. As a matter of fact, shortly after they landed, Winthrop delivered a speech that described why puritans were destined to be successful in the new world. He stated:

> We have taken out a commission … We have hereupon besought Him of favor and blessing. Now if the lord shall please hear us, and bring us in peace to the place we desire, then hath He ratified this covenant and sealed our commission and will expect a strict performance of the articles contained in it; but if we shall neglect the observation of these articles which are the ends we have propounded. The Lord will surely break out in wrath against us.[11]

---

[11] *Massachusetts Historical Collections*, 3d series. vii. 31-48 [reprinted in Robert Charles Winthrop. *Life and Letters of John Winthrop, governor of the Massachusetts-Bay company at their emigration to New England*, 1630. Boston: Ticknor and Fields, 1864-1867.

His message was clear. Winthrop warned the puritans that they had to do as God says to be successful in this new land. He continued that the Puritans were to, "Be knit together, in this work, as one man. We must entertain each other in brotherly affection. We must be willing to abridge ourselves of our superfluities for the supply of others' necessities."[12] His message was that God has chosen that "we the people" must be united together as a team so united that it is one entity because:

> … as *a city upon a hill*. The eyes of all people are upon us. So that if we shall deal falsely with our God in this work we have undertaken, and so cause Him to withdraw His present help from us, we shall be made a story and a by word through the world (emphasis, mine).[13]

Winthrop was likely the very first person who ever hinted at the fact that not only is America exceptional, but the people are also exceptional and that the whole world is watching. This sentiment would echo through history in many events, including the Industrial Age. After the Second World War, America declared itself the defender of democracy, as illustrated in John F. Kennedy's speech,[14] and later with Ronald Regan and his reference of America as the shining city upon a hill.

Other thinkers have also joined the discussion such as Sacvan Bercovitch, who in 1979 credits the Puritan ideological political theology as the main driver of the American Exceptionalism sentiment. Others, such as Henry Steele Commager stated in 1978 that he believed it was the European Enlightenment that paved the way for the growth of exceptionalism in the US.

---

[12] *Massachusetts Historical Collections*, 3d series. vii. 31-48 [reprinted in Robert Charles Winthrop. *Life and Letters of John Winthrop, governor of the Massachusetts-Bay company at their emigration to New England, 1630*. Boston: Ticknor and Fields, 1864-1867. 18-20].
[13] Ibid.
[14] President Kennedy's Special message to the Congress on Urgent National needs, May, 1961, John F. Kennedy Presidential Library and Museum

American Exceptionalism also started through feelings of nationalism in its infancy stages, as the United States continued to grow and defend its territory. What we know for sure is that what common folk thought about American Exceptionalism is not what it is today. America has continued to improve and get better, while its core foundations of freedom and individualism remain cemented.

As terms go, the "ism" gives away an ideological hint to what American Exceptionalism might be. However, the United States was not an ideology. Instead, it was the harbinger of a future that promised a democratization of Europe and other parts of the world according to De Tocqueville. At the time that *Democracy in America* was published, American Exceptionalism was mainly powerful, thanks to democracy.

While the idea of American Exceptionalism was first coined by De Tocqueville, it was Joseph Stalin's propagandist group who first made the term popular.

In 1927, Jay Lovestone, an American activist, and his colleagues discussed how America is socially and economically different from other parts of the world. Hardcore communists were bewildered when they found out that America is always ahead, despite not adopting more communist policies. It would take two years for Joseph Stalin to call his ideas "the heresy of American Exceptionalism," and that was the first use of the term. A few years later, when the great depression took its toll on the US economy, communists took the opportunity to double down on the crumbling of the US economy. "The storm of the economic crisis in the United States blew down the house of cards of American Exceptionalism and the whole system of opportunistic theories and illusions that had been built upon American capitalist "prosperity."[15]

The US was always known as unique, but the term itself did not find its way to the public debate until around the 21st century, when people tried to disapprove of American Exceptionalism.

---

[15] Brandon O'Connor, 2020, Anti-Americanism and American Exceptionalism: Prejudice and Pride about the USA, Routledge Studies in US Foreign Policy.

As for American Exceptionalism's popularity in the US, Ronald Regan was one of the first to bring it into the topic of discussion. Though Reagan did make American Exceptionalism more popular, his and his followers wrongly attributed the legacy of American Exceptionalism to the puritan origin. The phrase "a city upon a hill" gained a lot of discussion as the Puritans thought their society would be a civilization for everyone else to see that God would have the words of Matthew 5:14 come true: "Ye are the light of the world. A city that is set on a hill cannot be hid." However, what people don't know is that this phrase is no longer being used for its religious background, but as a political slogan.

Though Reagan saw the US as a nation with exceptional features, he never rallied the term or made it his saying. It was, however, used in the wake of the 9/11 attacks, as Bush explained how international terrorists tried to crumble American Exceptionalism.

Later in the financial crisis from 2007 to 2010, American Exceptionalism was more about its military hegemony than about its economical prowess, as the argument that America was economically superior and exceptional was much less convincing.

Nevertheless, the ideological orthodoxy of American Exceptionalism has emerged on a political level, which paved the way for critics and supporters of American Exceptionalism to debate the topic. The former president rallied for the idea that America was once exceptional but is no longer what it once was. Therefore, he called for reform but not revolution in America. Reform goes back to the idea that America simply needs to go back to what it once was, arguably a good idea since the United States was truly great, hence the slogan of Donald Trump: "Make America Great Again." The slogan sparked the debate talking point about America being great, or if it was ever great, and that itself has led many critics to pick apart American Exceptionalism.

There is no doubt that America has earned the respect of many countries as a pioneer of social movement, economic growth, and opportunity. America continues to champion human rights and innovation in the world. As author Thomas Paine asserted in 1979, the "revolution of America presented in politics what was only theory in mechanics." Since then, American Exceptionalism asserted that America was either or both distinctive, unique, exemplary, or exempt from the laws of historical progress. In reality, America was in no way shape or form behind in social progress, instead, it was leading in that area.

*   *   *

The absence of feudalism is certainly a talking point when it comes to American Exceptionalism and liberalism. Such things as hereditary nobility that is passed down from generation to generation is no longer the dominant way things work. Democracy and the people rule the country. The constitution cemented that idea by making no party of the government too powerful. The founders of the United States basically took everything that was bad in Europe and fixed it, and one of the biggest things to fix was the system of governance. Also, the idea of "tyranny of the majority" was never discarded by the founders, when they made the constitution, which is why states can make their own laws and regulation despite being under one common flag. As well, the USA, at the time of conception, had very little diversity due to its tolerance for diversity, no domination of the middle class, and a shared constitutional faith that united Americans and gave them a reason to love their country. Based on the above, American Exceptionalism would permeate every period of American history.

Republicanism was one of the biggest reasons for the start of American Exceptionalism, as the people no longer desired hereditary methods of passing down power. This was the birth of American Republicanism, which was championed by Thomas Jefferson and James Madison. They created what is known as Constitutional Republicanism, a system so unique, sophisticated, and effective in allowing the people to choose who they want to govern them, but not allowing tyranny.

While Americans and America have Christian values, this did not interfere with Republicanism and its virtues. Previously in Europe, people were ruled by kings who were seen as the descendants of God. However, the sentiments of the United States and its citizens are divinely ordained to lead the world to betterment still holds. Furthermore, the United States differs politically, socially, and morally from the Old World of Europe; and the United States is exempt from the "laws of history" that lead to the decline and downfall of other great nations. Nepotism was just one of the clues as to why not only does the United States challenge those laws, but makes the new version, i.e., Republicanism, even better. The entire world followed, and now we see that the most successful nations no longer have nepotism in positions of power.

While history does not actually repeat itself, it certainly rhymes. But in the case of the United States, we've seen time and again that those laws simply do not hold. Its exceptionalism is also true in the way history unfolds. Nevertheless, the idea of American Exceptionalism might lead us astray.

We've seen this sentiment with countless Americans who believe that it is all fine to strike another nation's army and blow up their bases, but if one American soldier is struck, the whole country weeps. The idea that "it's okay when we do it" is certainly questionable and needs further discussion.

The idea that the United States can do what it wants is not patriotism. The latter is simply the belief that citizens should support and praise their nation. However, American Exceptionalism holds that the entire world should bow down to the United States, and everyone should aspire to be like it. In contrast, patriotism is internal to a nation. American Exceptionalism is both internal and contains an expectation that it should be external. American Exceptionalism is something that is practiced, as we have seen in world affairs and the military. Not only does the United States generally get to do what it wants, but it also gets to decide what is good to do and what is frowned upon. It holds a clear sentiment that the United States is simply superior to any other nation. This becomes a downhill line of thinking, which is very similar to the way that White Supremacists believe themselves to be supreme. They think that their race is better, and devote their complete persona to the idea that they are allowed to do what they want because of a presupposed belief about the race of white people.

Americans who religiously believe in the idea that America is exceptional often get caught in a web of their own lies and questionable ethics, whenever America invades other nations and helps in the killing of many civilians in other nations. What was their response? "Freedom!" The United States was liberating those under a tyrannical rule. Notwithstanding, if this idea remains, or continues to grow, American Exceptionalism might become an ideology that would make the country a usurper.

CHAPTER 3

AMERICAN NATIONALISM

The concept of American Nationalism has been distorted and stained in the past few decades. The concept of nationalism itself has been warped and demonized; a term that was once used to describe pride and support of one's country is now deemed dangerous. This is especially troublesome as America is a unique nation and its nationalism is not rooted in race or the people. However, what is more troubling is the attack on American Nationalism itself has come from Americans themselves.

White nationalism is a term that describes a pan-nationalism that seeks to protect and develop nations with white Caucasians, in other words, a white ethnostate. Yet, the United States is certainly not an ethnostate, it is the opposite of an ethnostate. To remain consistent, America used to be a white nationalist nation because of the fact that founders and settlers were white descendants. America remained white for centuries, but after long fought political battles, America can truly claim to be a multiethnic country that sees people as not white, black, Hispanic or Asian, but as Americans.

White supremacy is a term that is often thrown around at white Americans who feel any pride towards their country. The misunderstanding is that since the United States founders were white and they protected white Americans, if you support these ideals then you'd be considered a white supremacist. In reality, White Supremacists are not very common, though they do exist. These people do not support America because America is a mix of races that recognizes everyone as equal. This is why White Supremacists are castrated from society and have not been successful; to be successful in the United States, you have to be American, and to be American is to support the American Creed, which is against racism.

CHAPTER 4

HISTORY OF AMERICAN NATIONALISM

The year 1776 might be the first thought when it comes to the birth of American Nationalism, but the true inception dates back to colonial times when a mixture of English, French, Irish, German, and European settlers gathered and united to create and protect the land they deemed home. Legally speaking, July of 1776 is when America became its own nation, but the events that accumulated to the pinnacle that is American independence defined the nationalism that is American. However, this term referred to the people who settled and protected the land, and it has been that way for many decades.

It was not until 1868 that the new 14th amendment was ratified to grant citizenship to all persons "born or naturalized in the United States." This was revolutionary as it included formerly enslaved people and literally anyone born in the United States. This was back when racism was not demonized; in fact, it was as normal as the morning paper. In the 19th century, the decision to include anyone in the United States as free and equal to anyone else redefined what it is to be nationalist.

Unfortunately, being a nationalist or patriot is still given the same connotation as in the 18th century. This narrow-minded vision of what being an American is like has polluted the minds of countless people. It is essential for nations to be national and hold views that aspire to make their nations better. The odd thing is that America has been built around nationalism for the longest time. America was great thanks to the unity people felt. If it weren't for the feelings of nationalism that transcend the physical, there would be no USA.

"America First" and "protection of integrity of our borders" urge Americans' self-interest before the goals of multinational structures. This is only natural and essential; the interest of the nation ought to be much more important than the interests of other nations. If a certain nation needs help from America, then it is obligated to recognize that America is already doing well on its own.

The sentiment of nationalism has been linked with racism by globalists such as elites, celebrities of media, and big businesses who thrive in a multilateral world that is actually dependent on the United States. Therefore, it is only natural they would desire less feelings of nationalism because that would limit the access they have to America and promote anti-Americanism. Those who stand against American values used the dichotomy of nationalism and globalism to compare with bad and good. It was easy to make people think that nationalism is bad because it is not in line with globalism, therefore, nationalism should be fought against. The latter is what many have thought and told the general public, and since it was globalism that had a huge reach, the battle for ideology was decisive and easily fought. Globalists made Americans despise their white nationalists, since most people believe that to be a nationalist is to be an advocate of your countrymen who are usually similar in ethnicity.

This all made sense after the Obama administration ended. It was completely normal and good to be a nationalist prior to what is to come; it meant that you cared about the welfare and future of your country and countrymen. However, during the 2016 elections, a big theme was nationalism. Democrats knew that Trump was rooting for the American people and their struggles, while Hillary tried to stand for everything including the United States and the entire world. She tried to appeal to conservatives, liberals, and everyone in between, which as some may say was her ultimate demise. Trump's approach was quite opposite. He was rooting for hard working Americans who were fed up with Obama's failures. This is politics 101. In addition, he heavily criticized over spending money on other nations and forgetting our own. American industry took a massive hit from international trade, which made labor cheap for mega corporations who outsource goods and services from abroad, yet hurt the American people. Political commentators were of the view that Obama believed in the idea that America is exceptional in a way that it is exceptional for helping other nations. Some would say this is why he was the largest spender among presidents by numbers, as he put the United States $8.5 trillion further into debt, while Donald Trump was the lowest spender by percentage according to the Office of Management and Budget.[16]

Supporters of Trump praise him by saying that he was a good president, which was reflected in the stock market, job creation, and even something that most people thought would not happen—he was the liaison for peace in the Middle East. He is also considered as the first president to not start a war.

Seymour Martin Lipset defined American Exceptionalism as, "Liberty, equality, individualism, populism, and laissez-faire economics,"[17] which, combining with religiousness and willingness, leans towards Libertarianism.

The Bradley Foundation regards American Exceptionalism as a set of ideals upon which America was founded that includes the following:[18]

- A political framework that favors individual liberty, limited government and the rule of law.

---

[16] Allan Sloan and Cezary Podkul, January 14, 2021, Trump's most enduring legacy could be the historic rise in the national debt, The Washington Post.
[17] Seymour Martin Lipset,1997, Review: American Exceptionalism: A Double-Edged Sword, The American Historical Review, Vol,102, No.3,(June 1997), pp.749-757.
[18] The Lynd and Harry Bradley Foundation, https://www.bradleyfdn.org/about/guiding-principles

- An economic system, which values the dignity of work, encourages innovation and embraces the pursuit of opportunity.
- A commitment to civil society and prosperity.

The argument to be made here is not that America should put itself in a bubble and shut itself from the world; rather America must work on itself and regard its growth and prosperity on a higher level, as opposed to working on policies that interest globalists. America has always worked with a global mindset and a prime example is its endeavor against the Covid virus that has plagued the US and the entire world.

On a national level, the federalist system ensured individualistic policies by each state according to what they thought was best, thanks to the checks and balances. The states adapted and had their own framework for handling the virus, while allowing the biotech and tech sector to look at new ways to work, educate and connect to fight against COVID-19. Americans also donated huge sums of money to more than 1,200 organizations around the world, in order to help many nations.

CHAPTER 5

HOW AMERICAN EXCEPTIONALISM IS DIFFERENT FROM OTHER COUNTRIES

What makes America truly exceptional? Is it the country's geography, natural resources or something different? The fact of the matter is such questions are extremely challenging to answer. If such a query were to be answered, this would mean there is an American formula, a step-by-step national tutorial that would lead any country to be held in the same regard as the United States. Such a task would undoubtedly be futile; what made American truly great is not a set of implemented policies or following a prophecy, it's the accumulation of its history, a shared goal and a unique story.

American Exceptionalism is based on the following basic principles: natural law, liberty, limited government, individual rights, checks and balances of government, popular sovereignty, the civilizing role of religion in society, and the crucial role of civil society and civil institutions in grounding and mediating American democracy and individual freedom. However, the belief of these principles is not exclusive to Americans, it is a shared belief that all people around the world ought to enjoy these principles.

At the time that America was founded, the shared dream was for a state that guaranteed natural law instead of dishonor, liberty instead of subjugation, individual rights instead of conformity, a limited controlled government instead of a dictatorship, sovereignty instead of subservience, and freedom. What really made this exceptional was that the US was the first country to actually fight for these rights and make them a reality. After defeating the British, who stood against every notion and principle the United States has fought for, it was true victory. However, the hardships that Americans had to endure did not vanish. The fight for American freedom continued for many generations. This is also considering the fact that the United States homogenized a blend of liberty, enlightenment, philosophy, and Christianity to embody all of these elements into one Republic.

As a country, America does not have a sole ethnicity, and is actually the first prominent example of a successful country that goes beyond a race or ethnicity. People from all over the world have come to live in America. So, if America is not defined by a specific ethnicity, could it be defined by its theology? That's another interesting thing about this country. While the United States is called a Judeo-Christian country, it respects all other religions and beliefs. Likewise, other Americans who hold different religious beliefs also respect the vision that America holds so dear. For instance, while there is a significant number of Jews who fled to the United States, they fully respect the way things are in an intercultural dialogue.

Not only does America present exceptionalism, it has also made other countries rethink their own nationalism. If a country thinks the same way as another, speaks the same, believes the same and has a similar culture, then what really makes that country special or different, other than its geography? Immigrants came to the United States in history in search of a dream. The United States was a place that all people wanted to go to because it represented a shared dream. Yet, America is not a stiff ideology, it continues to change and shift. Not only does America change the world, but American Creed itself changes the world. For example, during the time slavery was regarded as normal all over the world, the United States holds claim to the first country that abolished slavery with the 13th amendment, in 1865.

The concept of "all for one, one for all" is one that made America what it is today in the sense that Americans control their own liberty and destiny. However, American Exceptionalism is still not nationalism as we know it. The problem is that adopting the mantle of nationalism would weaken America's claim to being an exceptional nation. It would make this nation just any other nation, which is simply not the case. But, most important, it would undermine the peoples' claim to belonging to a nation that is grounded in principles that are universal—these are true not just for Americans, but for all human beings. American Exceptionalism is built on its founding principles, not cultural and ethnic differences, and that is the first step to understanding American Exceptionalism. Americans recognize their varied ethnic and cultural origins, but come together as Americans. This creates a nationalism that is no longer defined by a single cultural or ethnic reference under a government. Also, in the case of the American Nationalism, the government itself reflects the principles of natural law for every single abiding citizen.

The nation state is not what the American government used to create legislation, instead, it was natural law. The founders recognized the differences in language, ethnicity, ideology and in "way of life." America has also changed the style of government for other countries, but the democratic regimes that govern are nothing like the American democracy. Democracy is truly about what the people want, but American founders have also brought in concepts such as the Electoral College, administering two senators for each state, and an independent judiciary for what American founders have always feared tyranny.

The sense of belonging and patriotism in the United States is stronger than any other nation, according to a study done by Pew

Research Center. For instance, 71 percent of all Americans have described that they are very proud of their country, while only a third of citizens in Japan, France, and the UK say that they are proud of their country.[19] Americans also believe that they are truly the creators of their own density. Consider that a third of Americans believe that success in life is determined by forces outside of their control, but two-thirds of Germans and Italians, think that success in life is determined by forces outside their own control.[20] This also shows in the upbringing of future generations as 60 percent say that children should be taught the value of hard work, but only one-third of the British and Italians and one-fifth of the Germans agree with that statement.[21] In addition, more than half of Americans think that economic competition is good because it stimulates people to work hard and develop new ideas, while only one-third of French and Spanish people agree.[22] As well, Americans would like their views to spread throughout the world. Over three-fourths said this was a good idea, compared to only one-fourth of the people in France, Germany, and Italy, and one-third of those in Great Britain.[23]

American Exceptionalism sentiment has existed longer than one may think. Ever since the beginning of the United States, things have been different and better. In 1835, Alexis de Tocqueville noted there was much discussion concerning democracy and the rule of the people, and he stated there was a big commitment to values such as liberty, egalitarianism, individualism, and laissez-faire. He believed that there had to be something that sparked the people to

---

[19] Pew Research Center, 2014, Beyond Red vs. Blue https://www.pewresearch.org/politics/2014/06/26/section-9-patriotism-personal-traits-lifestyles-and-demographics
[20] Pew Research Center, April 25, 2018, "When Americans Say They Believe in God, What Do They Mean?"
[21] James Q. Wilson, 2006, American Exceptionalism, American Enterprise Institute, https://www.aei.org/articles/american-exceptionalism
[22] Ibid
[23] Alexis de Tocqueville, 1835, Democracy in America and Two Essays on America

believe in these sentiments and gave three reasons as to why this was revolutionary:[24]

- An isolated continent that is vast
- A legal system that got rid of nepotism and feudalism for the new Republic with a refined judiciary
- Embracing of certain "habits of the heart" that were profoundly shaped by our religious tradition

The American Constitution was also a revolutionary piece of documentation. The three first words that echo the values of the American Creed let you know everything you need to know when it comes American Exceptionalism: *We The People*. The Constitution resonated a sense of pride, diligence, each unity, and hard work. It recognized every one as Americans, no more special than the other. Even the head of the executive branch, the president, is not some godly, spiritual entity.

America also adopted values that seemed to be in opposition to what was going on in Europe. While kings and priests were trying to get local European towns to submit to a nation's capital, Americans were highlighting the importance of having a separate government, with checks and balances, so that no form of government can overwhelm the other, regardless of how little support it gains. This made old policies hard to get rid of and new policies harder to implement, i.e., creating a bill that moved to chambers of congress, then to representative sponsors, committees, and finally to voting. This complicated and time-consuming process was deliberately created, in order for every branch of the government to give its take on new laws and policies.

Many critics of the Constitution and the American Creed like to point to out that other countries in Europe have been able to

---

[24] Alexis de Tocqueville, Democracy in America, Updated: June 7, 2019 Original Nov 9, 2009, History.com Editors

implement social security programs, unemployment benefits, health care for all, and insurance much faster than the US. But the truth of the matter is that the presidential system, with a powerful, independent and internally divided Congress, generally requires that big changes undergo lengthy debates and substantive accommodations. Not to mention, the United States has always worked on providing opportunities to Americans, rather than having Americans rely on the government. The European parliament system makes much easier to change laws or the implementation of new laws.

The American system of law does not hinder progress, it promotes it. In a study that was done to see wealth distribution, political scientists Torben Iversen and David Soskice have shown that, among 17 large democracies, those that elect their legislators using proportional representation (PR), are three times more likely to vote than those electing them by majority.[25]

The divide this creates can be shown in the voting behaviors of countries such as Austria, Germany, Italy, and Sweden who have PR systems. Under a PR system, several parties will compete, while in majoritarian systems, only two parties usually contest elections. If there are several parties, middle-class voters will support programs that tax the rich and benefit them, knowing that they can change their voting habits, if a government wishes to tax them more. However, if there are only two major parties, middle-class voters will worry that voting for a leftist party will mean more taxes for them, and will be inclined to support right-wing parties.

When looking at American policies such as Medicare and Social Security that are facing an inevitable bankruptcy, we begin to learn that correcting an old program is as difficult as creating it in the first place. There is no doubt that Americans rely on these programs, but

---

[25] James Q. Wilson, 2006, American Exceptionalism, American Enterprise Institute, https://www.aei.org/articles/american-exceptionalism

there will be a need for a change that accommodates for the economy and the welfare of all American citizens.

The Constitution of the United States is one that guarantees the rights of people from various groups under one flag. This was expressed when Congress passed the Alien and Sedition Acts. After the US entered the First World War, the country experienced an overblown Red Scare; it took a century after the Civil War before Congress was willing to pass laws ending racial discrimination; and of late the Bipartisan Campaign Reform Act, written by Senators John McCain and Russell Feingold, constitutes a massive attack on the First Amendment rights of various interest groups.

The United States has been able to embrace immigrants peacefully with minimal tension, while Europe is facing the backlash of labor hacking. Labor hacking is a relatively recent strategy used by European corporations and governments towards immigrants from countries such as Turkey to make labor cheaper and revitalize its aging population. This worked relatively well for a few decades until it backfired with masses of immigrants coming into Europe with no intentions of assimilating, not to mention the refugee crisis.

The federal system that the United States uses is especially good when it comes to hearing what the people truly want in regarding policing, criminal justice, social issues, land use planning, schools, and other local matters, and more. The United States also enjoys a variety of policies of these agencies in a centralized democracy. Depending on the policies of states, counties, cities, and even districts, land use can be restrictive or liberal, school issues can be discussed, and other locally based policies can be changed. Yet, there are no perfect policies that guarantee freedom and equality for all people. Some states micromanage their residents' way of living accordingly, while others in the south at one time practiced active racial discrimination, which eventually called for a civil war. In other examples, locally elected school boards can often be captured by the electoral power of teachers' unions, thus creating a dubious bargaining arrangement: School boards that are supposed to negotiate with teachers over salaries and working conditions often are the captive of the very teachers with whom they must do business.

Federalism is not perfect nor is any other way of organizing countries. Economic strategies such as "the race to the bottom" from certain states that offer lower taxes can cause underfunded unemployment insurance programs. In addition, federalism can also block certain programs such as Roosevelt's attempts to combat the Great Depression and Obama's attempt to make health insurance accessible to more Americans. But there is no doubt that federalism has worked great for the most part in order to balance the powers and represent each state's interests appropriately, all by keeping policies close to the people. This was especially helpful when it came to governmental efforts in the 60s, due to the massive spike in crime in the streets.

Crime rates are also something that is dependent on the government. For example, back in the 70s, when England had less robbery and burglary rates, that statistic was most likely due to the fact England sent more people to prison, while California and other states had a loose system of jailing, and crime rates went up. Two decades later, the situation reversed, because America started sending people to prison more while England adopted looser policies.

Much like the city upon a hill, American politics and federalism is truly on display at all times and being held accountable. There has never been a shortage of public opinion concerning national matters, including from outside the country. This might be bad for the image of the United States, but it's a great way to get arguments from both sides.

CHAPTER 6

AMERICAN VALUES AND EXCEPTIONALISM

Fighting for freedom in the US has almost become a catch phrase. Ask any member of the Armed Forces who fight outside the country, and they'll tell you they're fighting for freedom. In fact, after the second World War, when America was truly crowned as a global superpower, Americans swore to protect democracy and freedom on their own soil and outside their country as well. This is something special and unprecedented in history.

Usually, when we see a country defeat another in warfare, they seek to further usurp its resources and perhaps destroy it. However, post-World War II saw a different kind of behavior from the United States, as it aimed to establish democracy and restore free markets in both Japan and Germany. In fact, the United States worked on the economic rebuilding of Europe, something that the Soviet Union tried to oppose. The United States spent more than $14 billion in order to rebuild Europe and refugees of the war which is equal to $260 billion dollars adjusted for today's inflation.[26]

Equality is also something that ties into American values and principles. "All men are created equal" is a reminder that no American should ever forget about their history including "life, liberty, and the

---

[26] John Brian Shannon, 2017, Who should pay to defend Europe, https://thisiseisenhower. wordpress.com/2017/03/19/united-states-defend-europe

pursuit of happiness." There have been many wars fought over this statement. At the time of independence in 1776, neither women nor slaves had the right to vote; what was considered to be equal were just men of European descendants and the founders. However, Americans knew that women, people of all races, ethnicities, and backgrounds had the right to be free and equal to everyone else. This is one thing that we can thank religion for, that all mankind is equal before God.

The United States is a nation that is truly forged in equality. In fact, America was the only nation to have a civil war over equality. At that time, Abraham Lincoln understood that equality had to be achieved and that America was the "last best hope of earth."

The Declaration of Independence also invoked all that is natural law driven. It started with something very basic and very simple and that is the assertion that mankind was inherently sovereign and dignified. In fact, the United States was the first example that dignified each and all person's choices and beliefs, and cherished such individualism. The founders, through experience and reason, looked at philosophy in Europe, drawing from the renaissance age and the enlightenment. English philosopher John Locke, 1632-1704, was one of the most central thinkers who valued liberty. Locke espoused the importance of government and a state where law exists; however, he disagreed with what many other thinkers asserted such as Thomas Hobbes who believed that "a place where self-interest is present and absence of any rights ... makes it impossible to form a society. It is a place where life is essentially anarchy." Locke noted that:[27]

It is evident that all human beings—as creatures belonging to the same species and rank and born indiscriminately with all the same natural advantages and faculties—are equal amongst themselves. They have no relationship of subordination or

---

[27] Thomas Hobbes Social Contract Theory Explained, Health Research Funding, https://healthresearchfunding.org/thomas-hobbes-social-contract-theory-explained

subjection unless God (the lord and master of them all) had clearly set one person above another and conferred on him an undoubted right to dominion and sovereignty. [28]

Though Locke believed that an individual's choice was dignified, he also asserted that mankind can band together to create a society to create mutual rights and benefits for all. Locke made these statements on the belief that man is free from any superior power or man's authority. Locke's views are a huge part of why America values an individual's freedom. The nation recognizes that no matter what, it is *unnatural* for man to be under the power of tyranny from another man. As Locke stated:

> The liberty of man, in society, is to be under no other legislative power, but that established, by consent, in the commonwealth; nor under the dominion of any will, or restraint of any law, but what that legislative shall enact, according to the trust put in it.[29]

Following from this statement, Locke maintained the importance for man to be more powerful than the government in general, but to be more loving for the "social contract." Clearly, this is self-evident in the United States. Americans generally have low views of people who are in control of government branches such as congress, presidents, and judges, but they have very high regard for the social contract that is the Constitution. These views by philosophers such as Montesquieu, Locke, and Jean-Jacques Rousseau were not considered to be viable at the time. The dominant hierarchy was too strong for people to revolt against the current state of affairs. However, the United States' experiment of human right and natural law proved to be very effective, and countries such as Germany, Japan, and Italy followed. Yet, centuries

---

[28] John Locke on "perfect freedom" in the state of nature (1689), https://oll.libertyfund.org/quote/john-locke-on-perfect-freedom-in-the-state-of-nature-1689
[29] John Lock, *Second Treatise of Civil Government John Locke* (1690), chapter 4, pp xx.

later, countries in the Middle East still struggle to gain a western style of democracy, just like the US has done throughout its history.

AMERICAN CULTURE EXCEPTIONALISM

The United States has dominated every major form of media and culture. Our consumer culture has redefined the way we people live and view the America dream. The nation exports all kinds of consumer goods, be it big macs, jeans, t-shirts, iPhones, cars, car parts, pharmaceuticals, industrial machines, and over 200 billion dollars in machinery. However, Americans have partly been responsible for web-based pornography, obsessive culture, and addictive platforms. This is not what the United States exported after the Second World War when it helped people in need. There is no denying that the consumerism culture has taken over the world as Europe, Asia, and some of the biggest countries buy into the vulgarity of American motion pictures and video games. In fact, Europe has taken a page out of our book and started doing the same genres.

The main sentiment around anti-Americanism is dressed up as a moral critique of America. However, most people who tweet about the ills of America are using an iPhone while snacking on Starbucks sweet tea. The capitalistic consumerism culture has created American culture and it is changing other countries around the world. America should instead focus its efforts in using the platforms it owns to promote public diplomacy, a love for freedom, respect for great talents, a willingness to forgo any imperial ambitions, and unity. This is exactly what the United States did after World War II. While we cannot keep reminiscing about how good the past was, we can always restore what made American culture great.

RELIGION AND THE UNITED STATES

Religion took an exceptional turn for the United States when the Puritans came to this land. These people fled from persecution due to the lack of religious freedom. This is why the religious side of the United States is exceptionally different from other countries. Religion has been used as a way to gain power from the people, but it was also used to limit power in many countries, such as in England.

In America, Catholics are Americans first and Catholics second, and the same can be said for other denominations. The debate over to what extent should religion be involved in making policies still stands. On the one hand, it has helped in abolishing slavery and giving equal rights to every American. On the other hand, it struggles to fight against abortion and war. Gay rights and other issues are also relevant in this discussion. It cannot be denied that religion can be dangerous, as we have seen with the horrific events in 9/11, the bombing of abortion clinics, and the inhumane treatment that gay people have faced. However, overall, there have been more positives with religion than negatives. People who are religious or believe in religion to some extent are more likely to contribute to their country's welfare. They are also more likely to form the nuclear family, overcome health problems, resist drugs, crime, and work hard for financial freedom.

Nevertheless, religion in the US cannot be the only way or the main way to practice Republican Democracy for a better future; after all, theocracies are hardly prosperous, and they can instigate feelings of animosity among people, leading to social upheaval. Religions might also become obsolete, or at least the practices of religion could become obsolete.

Another interesting fact about religion and the US is that almost two thirds of Americans have positive views on religion. However, around 62 percent want it out of politics according to a PEW research study.[30] There is no denying that religion plays an important role when it comes to the national sentiment of the American Creed, but it's important to understand that patriotism for Americans is more important than anything else.

AMERICAN CREED

The American Creed is the source of exceptionalism in the United States. It's something that is ingrained in the Declaration of

[30] Pew Research Center, *Americans Have Positive Views About Religion's Role in Society, but Want It Out of Politics* 2019.

Independence, a timeless and universal piece of documentation which united Americans on creed, not by blood. The American Creed can be defined as the shift of becoming American in every sense of the word. It is seeking opportunities, taking risks, fighting for freedom and respecting one's nation, flag and identity as an American. There are also major elements in the American Creed that include:

- Liberty
- Justice
- Equality
- Individualism
- Populism
- Laissez-faire

The American Creed can be represented in its symbols such as American flag, which stands for purity, justice, vigilance, and valor. It is a pledge of allegiance and a recognition of the natural law that can be heard through its national anthem. As well, industrial tycoons such as the Rockefellers, Carnegies and the Vanderbilts that saw the American Creed as a strength for morale to plant the seeds of capitalism, entrepreneurship and innovation in the gilded age. Though the American Creed had existed a couple of centuries earlier, it was more amplified immediately after World War 11 that America became a true economic powerhouse.

As strong as American Creed is today, it faces many challenges, such as the changing values of the nation, the diversity of beliefs, the polarity of political views, mass immigration, lack of assimilation causing a shift in American societal values, a growth of socialism and the growing tension between the United States and other countries, such as the communist Chinese party and Russia. Nevertheless, the biggest challenge is the lack of unity within the United States. Hence, America ought to strengthen its borders, not only the physical sense, but also the cultural and societal side to prevent the cultural degradation and degeneration of American values.

CHAPTER 7

AMERICAN CONSTITUTIONAL EXCEPTIONALISM

There is no doubt that America is exceptional in many ways. However, a big part of how it is exceptional and why it is exceptional lies in Constitutional exceptionalism. The Constitution of the USA is unrivaled when it comes to politics and history. Not a single nation comes even close to rivaling the values and contents of the American Constitution. It is also the result of long fought battles against tyrannical rule. When America was in its formative years, people in Europe dreamed of a future where they can be in a free nation that granted them the same right as any other. That said, the Constitution is the bedrock of American Exceptionalism as mentioned in the Articles of the Confederation: "the constitution, it may be said, is America's uncrowned king."[31]

THE STRUGGLE FOR THE CONSTITUTION

In more ways than one, the Constitution is the reward for the struggles that European people had gone through for centuries. The Founding Fathers were not only men of wisdom and farsightedness, they were also well aware of the struggles and desires of all mankind to be independent. With history as their guide, the Founding Fathers knew that

---

[31] Kelly et al, *The American Constitution: Its Origins and Development* Ch 6, pp 163.

the feudalism hierarchical system ends up with men stripped of their dignity results in further bloodshed and misery.

In their book titled *The American Constitution: Its Origins and Development*, authors Kelly et al. state, "George Bancroft in mid-nineteenth century wrote of convention work as the culmination of the entire development of all preceding civilizations up to the time."[32]

It was not an easy task to create a constitution that all people would agree on that also represents natural law. There was much opposition, including issues concerning the elections, the judicial powers, congress, central government, slavery, taxes, industrial powers, commerce, and the representation of the people. This marked the long debate between the federalists and anti-federalists, where federalist wanted to have the constitution applied as soon as possible and anti-federalists who opposed the constitution.

Federalists had similar views to John Winthrop, and realized the United States was a new nation at the time and needed a strong government as soon as possible. Domestic mutinies, inter-state rivalries, aggression from outside countries and other dangers were on the way. As Ralph Ketcham, Maxwell Professor Emeritus of Citizenship and Public Affairs at Syracuse University, states:

> They also supposed that the nation needed vigor and power in order to survive and exert its influence in the dangerous but opportunity-laden international scene. In short, the federalists sought English-style commercial growth, domestic prosperity, and world power, which they thought were compatible with Revolutionary ideals of freedom and self-government. They believed the new Constitution furnished the means for achieving those goals.[33]

---

[32] Kelly et al, *The American Constitution: Its Origins and Development*, Ch 6, pp 162.

[33] Ketcham, Ralph, *Anti-Federalist Papers and the Constitutional Convention Debates*, Introduction.

Both federalists and anti-federalists wanted one thing: to end tyranny. However, anti-federalists believed that a rush to create strong laws was a vehicle to create a hierarchical system where the government was a pseudo-king over other states and other people. As history proves, this could not have been farther from the truth. As historian Clinton Rossitor notes:

> The Federalist elucidates the kind of politics and constitutionalism that are needed in order to rescue the cause of the American Revolution and to vindicate the Declaration of Independence, which after all proclaimed not only "that all men are created equal" and "are endowed by their Creator" with certain unalienable rights, but that in defense of those sacred rights, good men ought to pledge their "sacred honor."[34]

The mental scarring drove the division between the federalists and anti-federalists. One side wanted the country to get on its feet and start trade to boost the economy while the other side was skeptical of the laws and regulations that were made. Ketchman stated that:

> ... the anti-federalists thought the goal of the American Revolution was to end the ancient equation of power where arrogant, oppressive, and depraved rulers on one side produced subservience and a gradual erosion of the self-respect, capacities, and virtue of the people on the other side ... Unless this cycle could be broken, Independence would mean little more than the exchange of one tyranny for another.[35]

There was very little to give when it came to compromising, and anti-federalists drew a hard line and did not want to go through the whole cycle just to end up in another tyrannical rule. Overall, it was very clear

---

[34] Rossitor, Clinton, *The Federalist Papers*, Introduction.
[35] Ketcham, Ralph, *Anti-Federalist Papers and the Constitutional Convention Debates*, Introduction.

what the anti-federalists wanted—a weaker government that can be changed and tweaked by the people, more representation for smaller states, and they favored Articles of Confederation. Their voices were heard and there have been many methods implemented in order to regulate the government to a point where both parties are satisfied. As a result, we have many practices such as the electoral college, equal representation in senate, and proportionate in congress.

George Mason and others believed that the Constitution was still lacking. It would start with a moderate aristocracy, leading eventually to the birth of a king who would make all these efforts worthless.

As a result, we can see the efforts of anti-federalists in the 21st century with less government, loose stronghold of central government, individual states, liberal democracy, more policy making for the strong role of states and protection of inalienable rights. Though it took months to ratify, the federalists managed to get the states to agree and move forward with the constitution.

Despite the lack of fanatic beliefs in religion, the Founding Fathers still had a fear of God and the higher power. However, greed, corruption, lust for power, materialism, and all of the fears that the anti-federalists had about the Constitution lined up against religious principles. This tug of war over the creation of the Constitution proved to be time consuming and troublesome, but resulted in the wonderful design that is the nation's Constitution today. The debates between the two parties can be reflected and seen through the give and take in the way things work in the power dynamics. No branch of the government is too powerful nor is it underrepresented. Nevertheless, the Constitution continues to face challenges, including race dynamics and injustices.

CONSTITUTIONAL ORDER

The Constitution of the United States may be an old piece of documentation, but it impacts the current state of affairs in the national news more than ever, now that the world is changing rapidly. As good as the Constitution is when it comes to giving everyone their opportunity and rights, political tensions are inevitable. Lengthwise, it is only around 4000 words with seven articles, but it still allocates powers for the three branches of the national government. It also speaks to the division of power between the national (federal) government and the states. At the time of the writing of the Constitution, the United States was only four million strong with constitutional paradoxes and inherent contradictions.

Slavery is a large part of why the Constitution needed a reform. Countless people called the Constitution inconsistent as it refers to "all other persons." There was a lot of debate and fighting over slavery and who gets to have the final say. Eventually, the United States did what it needed to do by abolishing practices of slavery in the country. However, this left the Constitution in a state where it can be reformed whenever. That said, the abolishing of slavery was not the end of all racism. It took a lot of steps from recognizing what's property and what's human. Republicans took it upon themselves to change the course of American history when they added the Thirteenth Amendment in 1865. Three years later, the Fourteenth Amendment would clarify terms of citizenship. But it wasn't until 1870 that blacks were considered equal to white men in voting. The Thirteenth Amendment stopped the tyranny, the Fourteenth Amendment gave blacks their national identity, and the Fifteenth Amendment gave blacks the choice to choose their fate.

Going back to the First Amendment, it is still something that's controversial. For all we know, the First Amendment is about the rights Americans have concerning free speech. It is the ability to express oneself regardless of race, religion, or color. The fact that the First Amendment can be micromanaged into small interpretations gave the judiciary the opportunity to tweak the law and bend the rules. Freedom of speech is considered paradoxical because we do not know the extent of free speech. According to author Sanford J. Ungar, free speech is not absolute:

Ironically, despite this unprecedented liberty of expression, never have Americans had a harder time figuring out what free speech means, or how to implement it with reasonable, common-sense standards, especially in higher education?[36]

While this was never the intent of the Founding Fathers, the judiciary has become arguably the most challenging and powerful of government branches. As constitutional specialist David Barton notes:

> In a simple overview, Article I of the Constitution sets forth the responsibilities of the Legislative branch, dedicating 109 lines to describing its powers; Article II addresses the duties of the Executive branch in 47 lines; and Article III has a mere 17 lines in its description of the responsibilities of the Judiciary …. implies that our Founders believed it to be the most important and most powerful branch, with the Judiciary the least important and least powerful.[37]

The discussion concerning the three branches brings forth their relationship and the dynamic among them. There are many instances when there is a power dynamic that grants the judiciary the same power as the legislative branch, and the same goes for the Executive. While some may see this as a perfect harmony between the three powers, it actually creates more vagueness in the way we interpret the Constitution. The same goes for the Executive Power, as we have seen in the case of Trump issuing a mandate to close all states early in February due to COVID-19, not realizing that it was not his responsibility nor was it his duty. Even when the president tried to bring back the economy after it had been battered due to the

---

[36] Unger, Sanford J. *The Paradox of Free Speech in America Today, American Council on Education*, October 17, 2018.

[37] Barton, David, *Original Intent: The Courts, the Constitution, and Religion*, 2011.

lockdowns, it was rejected by many. While his sentiment on wanting the country to get back on its feet was certainly patriotic, it was also unconstitutional. The Constitution has allocated policies on states of emergency such as pandemics, and they are there for a reason.

JUDICIAL ACTIVISM IN AMERICA

Judicial Activism has been one of the challenging aspects of the political arena in the past few decades. The way that the judicial system works is special, but it also leaves room for interpretation and law bending. The term Judicial Activism refers to the decisions and rulings of judges made on the basis of their personal views and political affiliations. While presidents and the congress have a fairly limited form of ruling, the judicial system can base their decision on the original intent of the framers of the Constitution or change those laws completely. This is definitely problematic for many reasons, as we have let the Judicial Branch solve problems that should have been done by the Legislative Branch, including civil rights, abortion, gay marriage, and much more.

In the legal dictionary, Judicial Activism is explained as: "Judicial Activism can take at least three forms. These include: the act of overturning laws as unconstitutional, overruling judicial precedent and ruling contrary to a previously issued constitutional interpretation."[38]

A lot of the situations when the Executive and Legislative Branch cannot operate are opportunities for Judicial Activism. This has been the case for a long time, since we have a polarity in the political scene. Traditionally, the Democrats have a majority in the Legislative Branch when a Republican is president. The same is reversed in many cases, with the Legislative Branch being mostly Republican when there is a Democrat president. But the Supreme Court is where the meat of the issue can be found. If one party could have a say on who gets to

---

[38] Content Team, 2015, Legal dictionary, Judicial Activism, http://www.legaldictionary.net

control the Supreme Court, there would be a balancing issue. Judicial Activism can apply or even create new laws. In these cases, the judges ignore speeches and laws by the Founding Fathers and even omit important documents.

Americans trust the Constitution, but the same can't be said about the three branches. This is why there was a lot of backlash every time the Judiciary Branch went over its legislative capacity. However, Americans must also trust those nine judges who are sworn to not go outside of the Constitution. Still, judges are human beings with emotions, but the Constitution is not. Any person, regardless of how stoic they can be, will show their political and/or religious affiliation when making certain decisions. Note that Article III, section 1 of the Constitution states, "[t]he judicial power of the United States, shall be vested in one Supreme Court, and in such inferior courts as the Congress may from time to time ordain and establish." This is what is used to bend the law a little. There is no defining limit to the "time to time," nor is there a definitive answer when it comes to "ordain and establish." Moreover, there are a lot of gray areas, which leave a lot of room for interpretation. The problem is that interpretations can often favor one side. This is a similar sentiment from experts such as Elizabeth Slattery:

> The role assigned to judges in our system was to interpret the Constitution and lesser laws, not to make them. It was to protect the integrity of the Constitution, not to add to it or subtract from it—certainly not to rewrite it. For as the framers knew, unless judges are bound by the text of the Constitution, we will, in fact, no longer have a government of laws, but of men and women who are judges.[39]

---

[39] Slattery Elizabeth, *How to Spot Judicial Activism: Three Recent Examples*, *The Heritage Foundation*, June 13, 2013.

The argument from the side that Judicial Activism is good is that the Supreme Court has to make decisions according to different ages, different demands and needs, which is true. The problem is that this could open pandora's box and leave a lot more room for interpreting in the Supreme Court. The original intent for the Supreme Court was not to make any laws and it was designed in the Constitution as the weakest to the three branches. In fact, they are subordinate to Congress, according to the Constitution, article 3, section 2.

Notwithstanding, the Supreme Court may also change the landscape of American law, such as in the case of Brown v. Board of Education, the abortion case of Roe, et al. v. Wade that changed the constitutionality of Texas from overstepping its boundaries. The case of Cantwell v. Connecticut was also decided by the Supreme Court in a groundbreaking case for the judicial history of the United States:

> In a sense, the Cantwell case is more important than the First Amendment because it gave the Supreme Court the power to control religion in the states. The Framers of the First Amendment did not do it. They wanted the states to be free to govern themselves. Therefore, the First Amendment begins with the word "Congress." By beginning the First Amendment with the word "Congress" this excluded state and local governments from its jurisdiction. Cantwell reversed this. In effect, Cantwell amended the First Amendment! Very few Americans are aware that the First Amendment was amended in 1940. But in a sense, it was.[40]

The tyranny of the majority is something people bring up when talking about the benefits of Judicial Activism. It can act as an anchor

---

[40] New, David W., *A Historic Example of Judicial Activism: Cantwell Case, American Pastors Network*, February 2018.

in many instances when the other two branches face difficulty. Contrary to popular belief, Judicial Activism is not a way to control other branches; it's a way to ensure there is a smooth functioning in government branches.

Other concerns surrounding this issue relate to the tricky way judges are appointed. Unlike presidents, judges can be selected by branches of the government. This is important because, in cases when the direct constitutional law cannot be applied and there is a need for wisdom, the person who calls the final verdict is responsible. Overall, there should be more Judicial Activism when needed. The real challenge and concern is regulating the justices and the process to be more constitutional and for the interest of the people. As Activist Sherry Suzanna states:

> Judicial review is a safeguard against the tyranny of the majority, ensuring that our Constitution protects liberty as well as democracy. And, indeed, the founding generation expected judicial review to operate as just such a protection against democratic majorities. A Court that is too deferential cannot fulfill that role.[41]

STATE CONSTITUTIONS

The US Constitution is a global outlier as it protects the rights of people through global standards, making it timeless proof of America's exceptionalism. Over the past two centuries, America would go on to make 50 state constitutions, and thousands of amendments and laws corresponding to the needs of American people.

There are three features of state constitutions that urge the reexamination of such policies. The first is that state constitutions are lengthy and meticulous. Second is these constitutions are frequently

---

[41] Sherry Suzanna, 2015, *A Summary of Why We Need More Judicial Activism*, Vanderbilt Law School.

reexamined and renewed. Third, state constitutions are classically devoted to education, labor, social welfare, and the environment, which are like most of the world's constitutions, making these legislations in the state constitutions keen on key issues that concern the state. The mechanism that state constitutions use is a defining feature of the principles as laid out in the Constitution, which emphasize flexibility and precision when it comes to law making.

The defining feature that makes American constitutionalism exceptional is the fact that it is not confined in the texts of the federal constitution. Therefore, one may consider that the American Constitution is the bedrock of American values with the state constitution being the ever-changing set of laws that stand up to the global standards and American needs. Yet, both constitutions cannot be separated from each other, as they should reflect the values of America. But, state constitutions are not free from criticism, as they have been labeled as unconstitutional since some states can ignore federal issues and they have been freed from the need to constrain their governments.

However, state constitutions share a similar design of the national Constitution; its mere purpose is to bear some of the weight that the national Constitution has to withstand. The United States is a much larger and more diverse country than it was in the eighteenth century and, therefore, needs some adjusting and amending for the policies. In fact, one may even argue that state constitutions seek to reinforce traditional values by accordingly adjusting to each state constitution. Further, state constitutions fix the lack of detail and the looseness of meaning that the national Constitution has, which leaves less room for interpretation while working on positive rights.

EXCEPTIONALISM IN THE STATE CONSTITUTION EXPOSED

One of the areas that seems to puzzle many people is the fact that state constitutions are needed, which apparently dilutes the national Constitution. One should rethink constitutional exceptionalism nowadays, as it poses a question of timeliness. The Constitution may have been a fine piece of documentation that quite literally changed America, and affected the entire world, but it is not as dependable as it had been in times past. Notwithstanding, the original Constitution has been nothing short of extraordinary and exceptional. State constitutions are indeed more democratic than the federal Constitution, as these documents have introduced rights and policies that guaranteed the freedom and rights of Americans in those states, such as the removal of property requirements for voting.

CHAPTER 8

THE MYTH AND THE REALITY OF AMERICAN CONSTITUTIONAL EXCEPTIONALISM

There is a widely held view that the United States constitutional rights jurisprudence is exceptional, and this is due to the long reign of American constitutional exceptionalism, in addition to the content and structure of the constitutional rights. As far as the content of the Constitution goes, it focuses mainly on brevity, and the high value given to free speech, while the structural claim is threefold. First, is that America has more of a categorical conception of constitutional rights when compared to other countries. In addition, the US has high regard for public and private decisions. Finally, the Constitution is a charter of negative rights that reject positive constitutional rights, including those that deal with social and economic issues dealing with modern issues.

The relationship between the state and religion is also something the United States Constitution has constantly dealt with, as there is a high level of church and state separation, with a low level of protection of religious freedom in a non-secular public and political culture. The role of faith is seen as extremely important. While being a Christian was never a requirement for being a president, it's hard to imagine a president nowadays with no religious affiliation.

CHAPTER 9

AMERICAN REPUBLICANISM

A big part of American values centers on the spirit of Republicanism that the Founding Fathers have fought for. However, one cannot help but think about to what extent this system of Republicanism has changed over the years. Has the country deviated from the original concept of Republicanism envisioned by the Founding Fathers? If so, how has this changed the social and political landscape in America's democratic, Republicanism system of government?

There is no doubt that Republicanism played a large role in influencing the US revolution, finalizing the Constitution, and making America the country that it is today. One question comes to mind is the nature of Republicanism and the Republican government. According to the documents of freedom:

> A Republican government is one in which the people—directly or indirectly—are the ultimate source of authority, electing representatives to make laws that serve their interests and advance the common good. A constitutional Republic, however, also limits the power of the majority through a framework that promotes competent government and affords protections for fundamental rights.[42]

---

[42] Documents of Freedom, http://www.docsoffreedom.org

Forefathers of America imagined a future for all Americans that would use this form of government in protecting the rights of Americans and setting international standards. The Federalist papers 10 and 39 are also helpful references in understanding the imagination and vision of our forefathers. For example, in the article IV section 4, the Constitution states that, "The United States shall guarantee to every state in this Union a Republican form of a government."

While democracy seems like the ultimate way to nullify and get rid of tyranny from the government, it might actually create more tyranny from the majority and leave individual rights unattended. This is what happens in a traditional form of democracy when there is no mechanism to check and control the majority party or faction against its excesses. In a traditional democracy, one group will thrive while the other will suffer. As well, traditional democracy might give people who are not responsible too much power, which can lead to chaos and division as long as there is a majority that supports them. This form of government always makes it nuanced, but what American Republicanism has done is basically weaken every form of government for the sake of democracy while guaranteeing individual rights. The legislative, executive, and judiciary branches, state governments, and the federal government are all there to create a system to guarantee social unity between the people and prevent tyranny.

There is no denying this makes the limits and roles of each government branch extremely complex and hard to manage with some forms of the government often overlapping. That said, there is no democratic system where there is no separation of powers. This was no easy task for the Founding Fathers as they engineered the roles of the government branches and defined the meaning of the Constitution. The forefathers had a lot of wisdom and knew that competition between branches is inevitable as the country grew larger, so they had to create systems of checks and balances to prevent excess of power. It would have been very easy to misinterpret the meaning of each clause and article, which is why the task of crafting roles for the government branches as an especially difficult task. Kelly et. al state that:

> Defining the nature of the executive, legislative, and judicial branches through institutional practice was the most important, if also the most perjuring, of the problems facing American political leaders. Other issues dealt with in the 1790s included the place of an organized political opposition in the constitutional system, the manner of settling disputes about the meaning of the constitution, and the proper relationship between the states and the federal government. Yet underlying these questions was the issue of the legitimacy of the new central government.[43]

It is important to acknowledge George Washington and his exceptional achievements. Many like to discard his role, but he had a huge challenge to face—to sell the Constitution and the federalist method of governing. For all the anti-federalists knew, George Washington could have been scheming in order to crown himself king of the United States. Thanks to his charismatic nature and decisive orders, he was able to protect his country and gain a lot of support. However, it still took almost forty years to finalize the system of checks and balances in a way that would prevent all tyranny and provide a smooth system whereby the government's sole role is to make the United States more prosperous. The task that our forefathers had was to create a system where every form of government can prevent the other from becoming too powerful. Initiating a Republican model of government first admits that pure democracy is potentially dangerous. However, letting the people decide what they want is still something that is essential. Constitutional specialist, SH Browne states:

> For now, on this day, in the first of America's first inaugural addresses, Washington held out the possibility that the "sacred

---

[43] Kelly et. al, *American Constitution; Its Origin and Development*, Seventh Edition, volume 1, Chapter 8, pp 115.

fire of liberty" might be sustained if the nation's leaders remained mindful that the Constitution was but an instrument of the "Republican model." In the end, the real destiny of the government it made possible could only be secured by the virtue of those to whom it was entrusted.[44]

THE UNIQUE MODEL OF GOVERNMENT

The Constitution provides for a very unique model of government that has allocated functions and powers to branches and members elected and appointed.

Presidents: The head of the executive branch that is responsible for appointing judges, ambassadors, government officials, and managing the government. The president can also veto legislation, grant pardons, issue executive orders conduct foreign affairs and command armed forces. *"Executive Power shall be vested in a President of the United States."* Article I.

Congress: The legislative branch can pass laws, impeach the president and judges. They can also approve presidential appointments, declare war, ratify treaties, and assess taxes. *"The Congress shall have Power To lay and collect Taxes, Duties, Imposts and Excises, to pay the Debts and provide for the common Defense and general Welfare of the United States; but all Duties, Imposts and Excises shall be uniform throughout the United States;"* Section 8 Clause 1.

Supreme Court: The judiciary is responsible for the last resort of conflict, but it is also responsible for interpreting the meaning of the Constitution and laws of Congress. In addition, this branch presides over impeachment trials, hear cases, and review the actions of presidents. *"The judicial Power shall extend to all Cases, in Law and Equity, arising under this Constitution, the Laws of the United States, and*

---

[44] Browne, S. H., *The Sacred Fires of Liberty: The Constitutional Origins of Washington's First Inaugural Address*, 2016.

Treaties made, or which shall be made, under their Authority;--to all Cases affecting Ambassadors, other public Ministers and Consuls;--to all Cases of admiralty and maritime Jurisdiction;--to Controversies to which the United States shall be a Party;--to Controversies between two or more States;--between a State and Citizens of another State;--between Citizens of different States;--between Citizens of the same State claiming Lands under Grants of different States, and between a State, or the Citizens thereof, and foreign States, Citizens or Subjects." Article III, Section 2.

The Republican model is still continually tweaked and changed today. However, is this model of Republicanism really the model that it was intended back when Jefferson made the changes to the branches of government? To what extent have we deviated from the traditional Republican government in the United States and do the elected representatives exhibit the required civic virtues for working for the common welfare of the people and our county?

Another important question to ask in this time is if we have a voice in the public policies of the government? The short answer to that is no, but it depends on what you define as a voice or having a say in those policies. In reality, the elected representatives do not possess civic virtues and they are not the embodiment of Republicanism. The relationship between government officials and the average American worker today is certainly not what our founders had in mind as they are completely oblivious to the issues that affect Americans which has caused an irreversible trust deficit between common people and government officials. It is safe to say that today we are living in a system of government that is neither a flawed democracy nor a shameful republic.

REPUBLICANISM IN AMERICA

The discussion of Republicanism is essential when it comes to discussing the ideological revolution of the United States. Throughout the years, it has played various roles in supporting the base of American values, but in recent years, it has played a renewed role in American constitutional thought.

In today's world, Republicanism is extremely underappreciated, even though it was this very ideology that made civilization what it is today. In fact, even current monarchies have devised a constitutional monarchy Republic hybrid, such as Britain and Sweden. This is relevant because monarchies have existed since 3000 BC, and reigned supreme for centuries. Only in recent history have we seen the disintegration of the monarchy system. While no one can tell if all monarchies will fade out, their decline was certainly around the time the United States was giving a lot of importance to Republicanism. As a result, this ideology became the counterculture and a form of a protest for the people.

The decline of monarchies was certainly foreseeable as more information was distributed and with the American Revolution, it was very clearly the people's time. Many experts actually argue that the reason why the French revolution was successful at the end was thanks to the efforts of the American people in defeating the British in 1781. The US would then go on successfully making strides in social progress, which led the French to believe that it was time they got their fair share.

However, Republicanism is not a counter to the monarchy. In fact, in some countries where Republicanism was introduced, the monarchy still existed and has even thrived.

Republicanism is not just a form of governing; it's a way of life that was more about eliminating kings and queens. It meant that Americans could set forth moral and social goals. The establishment of such people who wanted to create a society like that is not in and of itself exceptional; nearly everyone in Europe under monarchical rule desired to live with dignity. However, Republicanism in the United States gathered independent, egalitarian, virtuous, and ordinary people who wanted to be free from patronage and dependency on others. Republicanism also required those same people make sacrifices in the name of such a Republic. In the end, it required the sacrifice of countless lives, but their sacrifice was not in vain. Though they may not have truly believed in it, their sacrifices truly changed the world.

The ideals of Republicanism has been on a constant roller coaster, as the people had lost some of their spirit in 1787, with many starting to doubt and question their beliefs. Some people were in it for their personal interests and immediate satisfaction, others just wanted to invest in new land, but there were few who wanted to revolutionize the country. As well, it was often possible to exploit the popular electoral process and gain majority control of the legislature to pass oppressive laws that favored one party over the other.

There was a democratic revolution in the decades following the creation of the Constitution that transformed the tradition of classical Republicanism. In fact, it pretty much destroyed the dream of the classical Republic. Private political parties emerged in order to represent the interest of the people, and of course, people followed. As expected, this would inevitably cause some deviation in the plan of classical Republicanism, but it did allow the United States to come out on top of the economic and industrial revolution that would come in the nineteenth century. Nevertheless, much of the Republican tradition has remained alive, as the ideals of Republicanism stands for private wealth, liberty and the pursuit of happiness. Historically, Republicanism ranges from a representative minority or oligarchy to popular sovereignty. As Pulitzer Prize winning historian Gordon S. Wood states:

> Our beliefs in liberty, equality, constitutionalism, and the well-being of ordinary people came out of the Revolutionary era. So too did our idea that we Americans are a special people with a special destiny to lead the world toward liberty and democracy.[45]

The science of government is also something that Republicanism deals with. As someone with the knowledge of the second president, and

---

[45] Gordon S. Wood, 2011, *The Idea of America: Reflections on the Birth of the United States*

the vice president under George Washington, John Adams surely knew about the science of governments as he stated that "science of politics is the science of social happiness."[46] This attitude is arguably what made Republicanism successful in providing a system of governing that satisfies the majority, while gaining the approval of people like Thomas Jefferson, Samuel Adams, Patrick Henry, Thomas Paine, Benjamin Franklin, John Adams, James Madison, and Alexander Hamilton. This scientific approach to governing is what led to the social movements that seek to empower Americans, and is what led to the formation of the Republican party, known as red Republicanism, and its leaders such as Avan E. Bovay, Thaddeus Stevens, and Abraham Lincoln.

The ideals discussed were not a novelty; they had been introduced legally by Article 4 in the Constitution. American values are keen on liberty and inalienable rights, as well the sovereignty of the people. In addition, these values also reject the power of monarchy, aristocracy and feudalism, while expecting citizens to be virtuous and faithful to their country and in performing their duties. As Gordon Wood states:

> Republicanism represented more than a particular form of government. It was a way of life, a core ideology, an uncompromising commitment to liberty, and a total rejection of aristocracy.[47]

As well, Republicanism is keen on rights that cannot be repealed by the majority vote. This was one of the main concerns with pure democracy. If the majority can rule, then it can also crush the votes, needs and rights of other citizens. But Republican values introduced iron-clad laws that no matter what majority votes against, these laws

---

[46] Jeff Grimes, 2014, Historical Spotlight: Adams's Thoughts on Government, https://www.glimpsefromtheglobe.com/topics/politics-and-governance/historical-spotlight-adamss-thoughts-government

[47] David F, What Is Republicanism and What Does It Value, 2021, https://www.patriotsnet.com/what-is-republicanism-and-what-does-it-value

could never be broken. Therefore, Republicanism values human dignity and the pursuit of happiness of all its subjects more than the popular vote. Wood states that:

> Our beliefs in liberty, equality, constitutionalism, and the well-being of ordinary people came out of the Revolutionary era. So too did our idea that we Americans are a special people with a special destiny to lead the world toward liberty and democracy.[48]

One of the exceptional features of Republicanism is that America trusts individuals and their decisions, when it comes to governing. Therefore, they are the protectors of liberty. This is exactly why Americans believe in their system, as it presents the opportunity for every citizen to protect their own rights, be the creator of their own density and pursue their happiness.

While many like to crown democracy as the savior of western society, it should be Republicanism that we thank. In fact, Republicanism was the ultimate enemy of monarchies and it destroyed brute tyranny by monarchs. This ideology slowly but surely gnawed at the little trust that people had for their kings. Republicanism became more known in theory, but it became something that could be done in practice as the American Revolution showed. In fact, the American Revolution was more of a human revolution, as it destroyed the ideals that made society what it was.

Though Republicanism seemed like a goal that every country should head for, there was still some confusion as to what exactly Republicanism was and is. It is not necessarily a form of government, but more of a lifestyle and a philosophy that dignifies human life equally. It is "a form of life," as Franco Venturi has called it.[49] Sooner or later, any monarch knew their demise would eventually come, since people no longer believed that

---

[48] David F, What Is Republicanism and What Does It Value, 2021, https://www.patriotsnet.com/what-is-republicanism-and-what-does-it-value

[49] J P Ferreira, 2021, It is Time to Revive Republicanism, Cross Thought, https://crossthoughtblog.wordpress.com/2021/06/29/its-time-to-revive-republicanism

the monarchy were descendants from God or some celestial body; they knew that monarchs are just human beings like everyone. Therefore, many monarchies adopted a system of government where they could still call themselves kings and queens, benefit from the land they own, cement their legacy, and avoid the dreadful revolution. Republicanism seemed like a great idea. To add to the latter, defusing the monarchy would be a huge risk that could cause a revolution and an overthrow of the monarchy. Even Republic leaders knew that while people despised the way they were treated under a monarchy, they still enjoyed the charisma of the king. As David Hume, a Scottish Enlightenment philosopher, historian, economist, librarian and essayist, stated:

> The mere name of king commands little respect; and to talk of a king as God's vice-regent upon earth, or to give him any of these magnificent titles which formerly dazzled mankind, would but excite laughter in everyone.[50]

THE AMERICAN REPUBLICANISM LIFE

The task of securing the natural rights of Americans in a time of chaos was nothing short of extraordinary. The Republic was the best and the only way our founders could advance. In fact, one could even consider Great Britain to be a Republic with a strong monarchy. However, all these examples had their setbacks and flaws that were not an option for America. James Madison defined Republicanism as a representative government. It was more of a self-rule state than a pure democracy. Republicanism was a way to stop mob violence, dignify Americans, and create a rich land for prosperity.

There are a few characteristics that embodied the American Republic. The first was a "natural rights Republic" to limit the potential side effects of popular rule. In other words, a self-sustaining Republic where "life, liberty, and property" are sacred. The second

---

[50] Tom Macaman, 2016, In Defense of the American Revolution, International Committee of the Fourth International, https://www.wsws.org/en/articles/2016/07/14/revo-j14.html

is a "democratic Republic." While the folly of a pure democracy is a recipe for revolution, a democratic Republic is necessary. The Constitution itself starts with "We the People." Voting rights for Americans is what guarantees a democratic Republic.

Third is the "extended Republic." The idea of an "empire of liberty" was Jefferson's dream of a territory large enough to defend itself from powerful states and empires that ascend to power in modern times. A federal Republic is also another one of the six characteristics that can be ascribed to the American Republic. It must be unitary and ruled by a centralized government with enumerated powers. This is to ensure that the government, while unique and unitary, does not interfere with "the states or the people." This very point and notion, along with slavery, is what led to the Civil War.

Popular sovereignty is another element that was groundbreaking at the time of its conception. The new theory for American popular sovereignty dealt with the fact that people are all that mattered, and elected officials are their agents to whom they delegate powers.

The last element could be referred to as the "civic virtue," which is the standard of righteous behavior for citizens' involvement in a government. This is crucial because it relied on the people to make righteous decisions for themselves, and for the greater good, while the Republican government was responsible for protecting and defending civic virtues against the inevitable weakness of a fallen mankind.

The Republic is not without enemies. Liberty against power is a constant struggle needing to be tamed. Power remains a threat to stability in the government. This was always neutralized with the use of aristocracy or monarchy by having one reigning power overall. Nevertheless, Republicanism radicals in America altered that theory by rejecting monarchy and aristocracy, allowing the people rule themselves. However, this meant the government had to stay close to the people. This burden is what led to the form of government with emphasis on legislative power, written constitutions, separation of powers and scaling down the government.

The grounds for a Legislative government is the fear of the arbitrary rule and unfairness in judgement. A small Republic is also essential for durability and success of any Republican government, as the geographical challenges for a large country are plentiful. The written Constitution would serve to unify the people and their ideals, while providing a safeguard for liberty and against corruption.

CHAPTER 10

MYTHS OF AMERICAN EXCEPTIONALISM

American Exceptionalism has been a long-standing slogan for America for many decades now. This exceptionalism is rooted in the idea that America is fated to play a large role in the world arena that no other nation would attempt. This sentiment has been felt by John Winthrop and his group, politicians, presidents, and political thinkers, who either use the slogan of American Exceptionalism to excuse some of the behaviors that the United States has been questioned about, or to sell the idea of exceptionalism.

Political scientist Seymour Martin Lipest believes that this view is problematic as he states in his book, *American Exceptionalism, A Double-Edged Sword*: "Being an American, however, is an ideological commitment. It is not a matter of birth. Those who reject American values are un-American."[51]

America is rooted in liberty, egalitarianism, individualism, populism, and laissez faire. There is an equal number of thinkers who believe that America is not special, as there are those that believe America is exceptional. My belief is that America was certainly exceptional at one time, but the reason for its exceptionalism is not

---

[51] Lipset, Seamour Martin,1997, American Exceptionalism: A Double-Edged sword, The American historical Review, Vol.102 No.3 (June 1997) Oxford University Press

rooted in a cosmological plan created by God; rather, it was the circumstances that were given, and the opportunity that our Founding Fathers had, to create a nation that would become great. Additionally, I do not support the idea that since America is exceptional, it can be exempt from international laws and procedures. There is no doubt that America is at the forefront and leader of many issues, but that does not excuse any nuanced behavior.

The idea that the United States is special can seem to be too romantic and cause Americans to forget that the real reason why America was exceptional is because Americans worked hard and sacrificed for greatness. In reality, the United States, Britain, Sweden, Japan, China, and any other nation has something in which to be proud. Other nations have rejected the idea that America is great, and they ask, "How can any nation be exceptional? What would that do if that nation was exceptional?"

If enlightenment, liberty, equality, liberalism, religious freedom, freedom of speech, separation of church and state authorities, structure of government, war of independence, declaration of independence, history, constitution, separation of powers among the government branches of executive, judiciary and legislation, limited government, and other same sort of values and strengths make America exceptional and great, then why do these values and strengths, be it on lesser degree, not make other nations like Great Britain, Germany, Canada, France, Italy, and Sweden great and exceptional? In fact, some nations excel at these standards and can be considered as superior in every sense of the word. Every nation would be able to call itself exceptional and great.

However, America has volumes of arguments to call itself exceptional and these are just some of the favorites:

- The United States has more liberty and freedom than any other country of the world.
- It is the oldest constitutional Republic.

- It is settled by people seeking freedom of thought, speech and religion.

- It was found by people who were committed to individual liberty.

- Most statements of "American Exceptionalism "presume that America's values, political system and history are unique and worthy of universal admiration. They also imply that United States is both destined and entitled to play a distinct and positive role on the world stage.[52]

- America saved Europe and the world from two disastrous world wars, and humanity from nuclear holocaust during the Cold War.

- America is the technological mecca for students from all over the world.

- It has the highest living standards in the world, more opportunities, the largest economy, the highest GDP and the most powerful military.

It is argued that these types of slogans and attributes are just myths bereft of any reality, and all blunders and wrongdoings committed by America in the domestic and international arena have origins in these myths. These myths have been used as an excuse to violate international laws, individual liberties, human rights, and territorial independence of other countries. These myths include: America is different and exceptional power; it has responsibilities towards other nations as well. As Hillary Clinton wrote in her article published in Time, the "American nation is better than others, loves peace, rule of law and respects the liberty of other nations; all the good things are done by America as she has unique genius and God is always with them."[53]

---

[52] Stephan M. Walt, 2011, The Myth of American Exceptionalism, Foreign Policy, https://foreignpolicy.com/2011/10/11/the-myth-of-american-exceptionalism
[53] Hillary Clinton, 2020, Opinion | Hillary Clinton Says It's Different This Time. NYTimes, https://www.nytimes.com/2020/10/26/opinion/sway-kara-swisher-hillary-clinton.html

However, political analysts are of the view that the true past record of America shows that the nation has committed human rights violations, annexed territories of other countries, fought wars without any cause, destabilized different regimes in other countries, infringed upon their freedom, killed innocent citizens, intervened in other countries' affairs, and spent resources to fuel civil wars in different countries.

Critics argue that annexation of Arizona, California, Texas, and New Mexico, conquest of Philippines, bombardment on Hiroshima and Nagasaki, Nicaragua civil war, Vietnam War, Iraq and Afghanistan war, intervention in Libya, Yemen, Syria, Iran, and South and Latin American countries speak volumes about the hollowness of the claims Americans make. They are of the view that, while America likes to call itself the freedom country, it does not even adhere to that standard locally as it has the highest prison and jail population in the world.

It is argued that the record of respect for human rights is also not worthy of any admiration. America is not signatory to most human rights treaties and has a history of supporting and backing dictators and undemocratic regimes in the world. America never came in the forefront to support those communities that are being suppressed in different regions. The more surprising thing is that American leaders declare war against their so-called enemies with the conviction that this is holy war, and God is with them.

Political thinkers say that America is not even the first in economic freedom, and compared to the rest of the world the United States ranks number 12.[54] It also ranks very low for the freedom of press, life expectancy, literacy, child welfare, and quality of life. In addition, the US ranks very low in social mobility, which in an economy is linked to wealth distribution where it ranks 4th most unequal country in the world.[55]

---

[54] Mellissa S. Kearney et al, 2016, Income Inequality, Social Mobility, and the Decision to Drop Out of High School
[55] drhurd.com, 2016, Economic Freedom Ranking: USA No Longer in Top, https://drhurd.com/2016/02/04/economic-freedom-ranking-usa-no-longer-in-top-10

It should also be noted that the United States is not even the oldest Republic. In reality the world's oldest constitutional Republic is San Marino, a small country located in Southern Europe, which is older than the US by about 1,400 years. Even the Puritans, who were seeking a country where they could find peace in practicing their own religion, were hostile towards other countries and other religions. While it's true that the founders enshrined the liberties in the Bill of Rights, the Constitution intentionally prioritizes order above liberty, which was considered a necessary antidote to the chaos experienced under the Articles of Confederation, which maximized liberty. Regardless of the limits of freedom for white Americans, the liberty-loving Founding Fathers permitted people to be enslaved with the borders of their new country.

There is a common sentiment felt by the likes of Ronald Regan and even the Pope that America has some divine plan that will lead it to be victorious: "Into the hands of America, God has placed the destinies of an afflicted mankind."[56]

George W. Bush offered a similar view in 2004, saying, "We have a calling from beyond the stars to stand for freedom."[57] The same idea was expressed, albeit less nobly, in Otto von Bismarck's alleged quip that "God has a special providence for fools, drunks, and the United States."[58]

Another myth around the exceptionalism of the United States is that the Founding Fathers hold special genius and brains of superheroes. Their belief is that the Founding Fathers had God-like powers that allowed them to be exceptional and create a country that was exceptional. However, it was not until the following century that

---

[56] 'Into the Hands of America': Pope Pius XII's Blessing, National Catholic Register, shttps://www.ncregister.com/commentaries/into-the-hands-of-america-pope-pius-xii-s-blessing
[57] Otto von Bismarck. goodreads, https://www.goodreads.com/quotes/95610-god-has-a-special-providence-for-fools-drunkards
[58] Walt, Stephen, M, *The Myth of American Exceptionalism, Foreign Policy*, October 11, 2011.

the issue of slavery was fixed. In fact, that issue of slavery alone is one of the worst stains on American history. As Kelly et. al noted:

> The constitution convention confirmed the character of slavery as a local institution. Although it might be argued that recognition of slavery in the constitution made it in some sense a national institution, the framers' chief purpose in this regard was to affirm state rather than federal power over the institution.[59]

While the argument that slavery was very difficult to get rid of—considering the majority of the Founding Fathers themselves owned and traded slaves—according to the critics, it showed shortsightedness from the side of Founding Fathers who were not able to give equality to slaves. Historian Matthew Spalding states, "In the way our Fathers originally left the slavery question, the institution was in the course of ultimate extinction, and the public mind rested in the belief that it was in the course of ultimate extinction."[60] Spalding also quotes Abraham Lincoln who observed in 1858, "All I have asked or desired anywhere, is that it should be placed back again upon the basis that the Fathers of our government originally placed it upon."[61]

The merits of American Exceptionalism rest on different matters and these are the great military power, the strong economy, advanced war technology, constitutional exceptionalism, a unique checks and balances system, federalism, decentralization, judicial system, philanthropy, equality, justice, and religious freedom. There is no denying that America has these and is exceptionally superior in these areas. A proof of this is the flood of immigrants who would give an arm and a leg to come to the United States. Let's face it, the United States is exceptional at treating people well, as everyone is granted

---

[59] Kelly et al, *The American constitution: Its Origins and Development*, Chapter 14, pp 242.
[60] Spalding Matthew, *How to understand slavery and the American founding*, Heritage Foundation, August 26, 2002.
[61] Ibid.

equal opportunities, protection, fair judgment, freedom, property rights, and a vast economy. As well, being an American is not about race or religion, it's about having a shared dream. Moreover, the United States is a country that has successfully weaved people from all cultural backgrounds into the strong economic fabric. Finally, the United States has been exceptionally good at peace and collaboration.

Nonetheless, intellectual circles opine that if we held America at those standards, it's safe to say that it no longer meets those requirements and has lost its exceptionalism. This is evident in the social division, political conflicts, fanaticism, hatred, animosity, diversity, racial discrimination, and economic downfall. Today's current issues are leading to the worst job opportunities for Americans, illegal immigration, weak borders, health care issues, a stark decline in marriage, a weak education system, welfare, and a loose budgeting strategy that is slowly leading to crippling debt. It is now time that we stop the nostalgia or the delusion of American Exceptionalism and start revisiting history, how America became great and work on rebuilding the values that can make it exceptional.

CHAPTER 11

AMERICAN EXCEPTIONALISM AND FOREIGN POLICY

The foreign policy of a nation often mirrors their success on a global scale and the stance that a country takes nationally. It revolves around national economic and security interests, and can play a large role in the protection of that nation's citizens around the globe. For a country like the United States, foreign policy is especially important, since America has a strong military and a history of standing for peace. Though the US plays a critical role in global foreign relations, the engagements involving the United States often led to more of a conundrum.

The question that many Americans ask is why does an event happening in Bangladesh, Pakistan, or India matter to the USA, and why should we care, after all, aren't they continents away? The reason why the US is involved in these issues is because foreign issues often become domestic issues. The world is such an interconnected place that any event in the world will likely affect our daily lives. All of these events trickle back, and they can be as minor as showing up in the news, as important as getting called up to serve in the military, or as critical a spike in gas prices.

Foreign policy refers to the way we connect with other countries, including commerce, peace relations, technology, manufacturing, art, media, culture, sports, and academia. Americans are affected by the country's foreign policy more than other nations because they are by nature more isolationists, live in a world according to their values and traditions. But this did not last long; the US has been in and out of foreign policy since its creation but has become the main topic of discussion after the Second World War. America took it upon itself to protect freedom and liberty around the world and has since become less isolationist.

One thing has been clear surrounding the foreign policy of the United States around the world, it seeks to stop the massive spread of communism. The United States realized there is an ongoing threat that was bigger than Germany during the Second World War, and that was the USSR. Political analysts argue that the threat of nuclear weapons, the allegiance with newly formed countries, and the military supremacy of communism were not just a threat to the United States, they were a threat to the entire world. This was why the United States fought wars with Vietnam and Afghanistan. However, many people disagree with the stance the United States takes on foreign policy and calling itself the world's policeman. Within the nation, one party believes the United States should withdraw troops and focus on national and local matters, while the other party, mainly proponents of liberal internationalism, believe that America should play its role in international peace and use brute force when needed to maintain peace.

A prominent proponent of idealism in recent times is George W. Bush, who expressed the idea succinctly when he said, "It is the policy of the United States to seek and support the growth of democratic movements and institutions in every nation and culture, with the ultimate goal of ending tyranny in our world."[62] Bush used the idea that the United States should focus on the security of our nation, but that was in theory. Practice was a different story, as he believed that

---

[62] Jorge Dominguez, 2015, Introduction: Bush Administration Policy, ReVista, https://revista. drclas.harvard.edu/introduction-bush-administration-policy

"we have a greater objective than eliminating threats and containing resentment. We seek a just and peaceful world. This goal—ending tyranny across the globe and establishing a just and peaceful world—is the aim of idealism."[63]

The proponents of realists believe the United States should focus on foreign policy as long as it's related to national interests and not moral principles. Therefore, national interest should come out on top all the time when talking about foreign policy. As long as the foreign relations can bring the country some gain, be it manufactured goods or more services, the United States can engage in foreign policy.

Talking about this is extremely important. Wars are very costly, not just monetarily, but also in the cost of lives. Moreover, it has caused economic downfall and recession. Fast forward to 2011 and the outside threat became even louder. In fact, it even became local. Consider that:

> The events of September 11, 2011 brought home to America the realization that retreat to a fortress America, the recurring isolationist approach to foreign policy in American history, is no longer (if it ever had been) a realistic option. The ongoing threat of massive terrorism cast this country into the maelstrom of world conflicts suddenly and to a degree for which the nation was quite unprepared and unwilling to support on a long-term basis.[64]

The discussion around foreign policy during the threat of terrorism under "War on Terror" was more about just the war on terror. In fact, it was an ideological war to gain power and control over the annexation of oil wealth in the Middle East. The attack on

---

[63] Craig Biddle, *US Foreign Policy: What's the Purpose, The Objective Standard*, May 21,2015.
[64] Cochran et al, Chapter 12, pp 435.

Afghanistan was done under the excuse of the 9/11 terrorist attacks. However, it served other areas, such as keeping an eye on Russia, China, Iran, and Pakistan. After keeping its troops in Afghanistan for twenty years, USA withdrew without any apparent or declared plans leaving Afghanistan in turmoil. The Afghan war caused huge human and economic loss to America.

The issue of Palestine is also something the United States barged into, although the Palestine conflict has been going longer than just the Egypt-Israel-Palestine conflict in 1947. America should play a decisive role to resolve this issue once for all so both Palestine and Israel may live peacefully and independently on their homelands. Both Israel and Palestine will have to learn to coexist as good neighbors and open hearts for each other to live peacefully. Israel still has many enemies that are very close geographically, such as Egypt, Turkey, Iran, Jordan, and Syria. Notwithstanding, America has a long history of wreaking havoc in the world whenever it enters conflict.

The United States was in every sense of the word the strongest and most powerful nation in the world after the fall of the USSR in 1989, and the United States has taken that role in culture, military, technology, science and research. In fact, the US has been at the forefront of these areas for decades. This sparked the debate of whether or not the United States should focus on domestic issues, or act as the policeman of the world.

On the one hand, the United States can strengthen its foundations, empower its people and build unrivaled industries; on the other hand, it can play a moral and ethical role in promoting human rights. There are many facets to this argument, as evil will always exist and conflict will always exist. The United States can control some of these conflicts, but history shows that they have often ended in more bloodshed, so should it really be at the forefront of these issues? Yes, America maintains hegemony by entering these conflicts, the leadership of the US has granted it to be a leader in world politics, but there are emerging forces such as China who excel militarily and economically. There is a strong belief among political analysts that America is slowly but surely losing its spot as the poster child of freedom, equality, economy, and foreign policy.

FOREIGN POLICY EXCEPTIONALISM

The culture of politics in America maintains a missionary character that extends to help others for the sake of promoting American values in other parts of the world. There are a few reasons why this belief still stands. The first is that Americans believe they have an exceptional creed that drives them as a people on a mission. We can date this back as far as the 16th century, when John Winthrop and his group called America "a city upon a hill." This sentiment has existed ever since, and even today, Americans feel that they are different from the rest of the world.

Americans are also fond of the idea that they are in the New World. The main concept behind this is that America is the New World that will grant its citizens freedom, morality, dignity, and global power. The other belief that Americans have that shapes the foreign policy is that America isn't going to follow the course of history like Europe did, which is going to save it from the demise of great nations. China, as an example, was a powerhouse when it was thriving, but its isolationist policies and trade behavior in the 1500s is what crushed the Chinese dynasties. Some believe the British had caused China's collapse, but in reality, China should have easily defended against the British troops, given the number of resources and power they once had.

There are other reasons that contribute to American Exceptionalism character in foreign policy, such as the moral high ground and the pathological altruism for promoting freedom in the whole world.

All things considered, we are now well aware that America regards itself as exceptional, and other countries think the same. This is what caused the American identity to have played an important role in its foreign policy behavior. This identity has a dichotomy of exemplary and missionary exceptionalism. It attempts to make the world a safer place for democracy and freedom, but it also wants to set a standard that is exemplary. Consequently, America is shouldering the responsibility of the leadership of western civilization to keep it safe and free from threat.

It is important to remember that American Exceptionalism is an ideology that encompasses the transfer of the American Creed to the outside world. This idea dominated American foreign policy in the era of the Cold War, which amounted to a battle between the exceptionalism of the United States and the violent spread of the USSR, all within the battlefield of Asia and Europe.

THE TIMELINE OF AMERICAN FOREIGN POLICY

To understand United States diplomacy better, it is important to look at the past. The United States started off in need of the world; the government had spent billions on the military and had a lot of debt. Overall, the United States would not play a major role in world politics until around the First World War, and more notably after the Second World War. This time period was referred to as isolationism. The United States clearly isolated itself as it promised to stay away from European matters and warned Europe about coming to the US. The end of isolationism started when America gained control over Puerto Rico and the Philippines. It also annexed the Panama Canal and gained control over Hawaii. America tried to remain a neutral country for three years in the First World War, but eventually quit that promise after it declared war on Germany, due to the attacks on American ships.

After the First World War, the United States swore to remain isolationist and remain neutral under Roosevelt. Once again, this took a different turn when Japan bombed Pearl Harbor, Hawaii, on December 7, 1941. After the war, the US, Britain and the Soviet Union emerged as victors. However, the US and USSR came out as the two superpowers in the world. This also coincides with globalism, as the United States aimed to protect its interests around the world using its military power.

The USSR and the United States had clear differences between them, such as one side favoring communism and command economy while the other favored democracy and free enterprise, thereby creating what was called the Cold War. The United States feared that communism would take over the world, and feared a nuclear war which, at times, was very close. Under Truman, the exceptionalism of the United States endeavored to help other countries that were struggling against communism. This is also when the United States helped create NATO and rebuilt the economy of countries that struggled after the war. Containment would come, thereby causing the spread of communism in Vietnam and the separation of Korea into the north communist region and the south liberal region. Communism was and is brutal, and it was only a matter of time for the USSR to crumble to the ground. The Cold War ended with the fall of the Soviet Union, but some countries still struggle due to their communist background.

When the Soviet Union collapsed in 1991, the United States became the world's sole superpower. At the time, many people foresaw "the end of history." Democracy and peace, as they predicted, would sweep across the globe. It didn't turn out that way, of course, and some say that's because the U.S. is shirking its responsibilities.

What is more is that the initiative taken by the US military is still as active as it was involved in the Gulf war. During that time, America established its access to oil in the Middle East.

The United States was not free from problems in its own turf around the 90s. Many Americans began questioning the American foreign policy. However, the attacks on the Twin Towers renewed the desire for foreign policy, as international terrorism became the new threat to America.

Looking ahead at the future, American foreign policy is especially important as Joe Biden takes the president's office. America can no longer claim that it is the absolute best at everything. The economy of the United States is declining, and the military has weakened, due to international responsibilities America has taken. China, on the other hand, is slowly growing its army at a steady rate, and establishing a world-level threatening economy that some call the strongest economy today. Pandemics and wars usually cause the worst financial downfall in nations, and we have seen China takes the pandemic threat on the chin and appears to have already recovered from the damage. In fact, China is taking this opportunity to establish an even more impressive and robust economy, military and superior international trade position, and it has a desire to secure the mantel of exceptionalism. As notable historians, Elbridge Colby and Jim Thomas, state:

> No other like-minded country is strong enough to perform the United States' leadership role in this alliance network. The United States is the only nation with the power, global reach, financial depth and standing to cohere and maintain such a diverse grouping for broadly liberal ends...[65]

THE POLITICS OF FOREIGN POLICY AND AMERICAN EXCEPTIONALISM

While visiting troops in Iraq, Donald Trump said Washington will no longer play the role of the "world's policeman." But no one can replace the US — not even the EU.[66] The vast majority of Americans believe that the United States should protect America and stay away from unneeded international conflict. It's important to talk about the divide in this discussion because the two groups who have this dichotomy are the two dominant parties in the US. Nevertheless, they are still on the cuff for Wall Street, the military industry, AIPAC and other large interests. While the left feels betrayed by their party and the same goes for the right, Americans feel betrayed by both.

The country is now facing the largest and greatest constitutional crisis in over two centuries, with a wild power dynamic that is putting

---

[65] Elbridge Colby and Jim Thomas, 2016, The Future of Alliance, The National Interest, No.144, (July-August 2016).
[66] Christoff Hasslebatch, 2018, Opinion: No country can replace US as world police, DW, https://www.dw.com/en/opinion-no-country-can-replace-us-as-world-police/a-46894590

imperial presidency and Congress in the grey area. The race to the bottom has never been worse as Republicans failed to pay more taxes for the welfare state, and the Democrats raise taxes causing an exodus in some of the most lucrative economic hotspots in the country. In short, regardless of the party's economic platform, both Republicans and Democrats compete to be fiscally irresponsible. The country is now facing trillion-dollar annual deficits and uncontrolled spending. A financial crisis is drawing near due to thoughtless spending, shadowed by weak international foreign relations. In retrospect, the founders believed that defending the borders and maintaining an active democracy was more important than an aggressive military. In other words, the core of American Exceptionalism calls for a noninterventionist foreign policy.

PART THREE

THE FUTURE OF AMERICAN EXCEPTIONALISM: A LOOK FURTHER AHEAD

INTRODUCTION

Exceptionalism in the United States has created a lot of talk and debate over the last few years. In the past century, America barely had a moment to catch its breath from fighting in wars to protecting other people in other countries and establishing more security in fear of terrorism. However, now that the world is arguably more peaceful than it has ever been overall, with no looming threats militarily, it is time to reconsider some decisions and rethink about the notion of America first. The economic, social, and foreign structure of the United States needs to be revisited. As the world is moving rapidly forward these days, "We The People" are in charge of this country and it is our responsibility to protect the values of what made America great.

AMERICAN EXCEPTIONALISM: A REVIEW

Ever since the United States of America was founded, Americans have been bombarded with the typical slogans, rhetoric, references, and statements to convince the nation, and other nations, that the USA is an exceptional and different, with a unique and important role to play in the world arena. The United States set the standards for itself to be the best nation in the world, one that is also destined to be the greatest. This American discourse has been broadcast in books, newspapers, treaties, TVs, radios, movies, telegrams, and even in the current folk culture by politicians, presidents, political thinkers, and professors who seek to find an excuse to promote their ideologies, or excuse what the United States has done in the past.

However, this rhetoric is a double-edged sword according to many contemporary thinkers around the world. It is the commitment to unbelievable standards, an ideological commitment that is simply impossible to meet in today's world. In addition, American Exceptionalism simply does not do anything other than charging the United States with a burden to be better than any other nation, but it does not promote any real change. American Exceptionalism connotes that the United States is a country that is exceptional regardless of what it does, hence the term American Exceptionalism.

Right now, the United States is a nation that does not champion all of its values. For instance, the United States has the highest concentration of jailed individuals. It might be a country full of opportunity, but it's not the only one, and the nation has fallen down when it comes to its values in the past few years. The idea that America is exceptional has evolved with time, but in today's age, that notion of exceptionalism has devolved, since it has mainly a negative sub context.

The fact is, the United States was at some point exceptional. During second half of the 20th century, the United States championed universal human rights and was the main leader in creating the Universal Declaration for human rights. In addition, the United States participated in the Nuremberg International Military Tribunals, which was the first global group that prosecuted people for breaking the laws of universal human rights. Moreover, the United States has created the "law of the seas," which is a system that promotes legal trading that has been arguably one of the biggest reasons for global prosperity.

When it comes to innovation and creating machinery, the United States has been the leader for the last 80 years. In fact, the United States has been the overwhelming inventor of goods such as the Internet, computers, GPS, chemotherapy, mobile phones, laptops, the modern suspension bridge, the light bulb, the photographic film, the first skyscraper, the first airplane, microwaves, the first space shuttle, and the list goes on. Anyone who attempts to promote the demagoguery that the United States is overrated or anything less than spectacular is either a biased or uneducated.

All of these achievements on America's records are thanks to its values. The values for freedom, opportunity, equal rights and daring to be great are arguably why the United States holds the mantle for achievements in science and technology.

Now we know the baseline and where we need to set the standards and what ought to be done. Americans must instill the values that made America the greatest country on earth because these values transcend time and space.

The last section of this book will deal with how the last embers of exceptionalism are shaping up to be. What this section will aim to tackle is to expose the dichotomy of whether or not American Exceptionalism should be restored or changed. Is it truly no longer America's time, or can the United States make a comeback?

CHAPTER 1

AMERICAN EXCEPTIONALISM: RESTORATION FOR THE ECONOMY

It is no secret that the economy of the United States is in dire straits, which can be observed by the colossal amounts of debt the country is building up, brain drain and the outsourcing of goods and services outside the US. Unemployment rates have skyrocketed, and the pandemic is truly showing how fickle the economy is. The dollar is weakening, people are having to work more hours or more jobs, the price of food, gasoline, and other necessities is rising, but the value Americans are getting in return is decreasing. However, this is not due to the global weakening of the economy; it is due to the volatile system of government the United States has. The answer is simply the government is making people rely on it too much, and the system is too slow in responding and destroying the habits that made America exceptional in its economy.

The welfare state was a great initiative to create a more stable economy and fair grounds for Americans after the Gilded Age. Business was booming between 1890 and 1912, so the government decided that it would regulate the private economy. The professionalization of the government promised that it would curb the worst side effects of capitalism and benefit from the fruits that come from that economic system. This came in handy during the Great Depression, since the government provided benefits in health for Americans. Three decades later, these programs would become more sophisticated with food stamps and Medicare. As the population of the United States grew, so did the population's dependency on those programs, which required a large bureaucracy to govern and has evolved into what we now have— a welfare state. However, the creation of the welfare state has proven to be inappropriate for an economy like the US, and issues such as bankruptcy are just one example.

Social security for example is a system that was created back when there were a lot of jobs. In fact, there were 42 workers for one retiree.[67] That ratio is very different now with three workers for one retiree.[68] In the 1960s, Lyndon B. Johnson promised the war on poverty would be a winning one and it was. However, six decades and over 20 trillion dollars later, the welfare system seems to face a dead end that does not benefit the poor in any way but hurts the life of average hard-working Americans. According to a federal government census, 12 percent of Americans are poor and this is still a reality, despite the fact that the federal government spends over one trillion dollars every year in dozens of welfare programs.[69]

Lyndon B. Johnson's original intent was not to increase the dependence on government; in fact, he wanted less dependence. He also wanted Americans to depend on their efforts and work ethics to get them out of poverty, and his goals should remain today. However, what we are seeing is the complete opposite.

---

[67] John Stossal,2010, Obama Demagogues Private Enterprise, Town Hall, https://townhall.com/columnists/johnstossel/2010/08/18/obama-demagogues-private-enterprise-n744138
[68] Veronique de Rugi, 2012, How Many Workers Support One Social Security Retiree? Mercus Center, https://www.mercatus.org/publications/social-security/how-many-workers-support-one-social-security-retiree
[69] Emily A. Shrider et al, 2021, Income and Poverty in the United States: 2020, Report Number P60-273, United States Census Bureau.

The main flaw in today's welfare system is very clear; it discourages the very things that get rid of poverty: marriage and work. It is common knowledge that work and marriage raise incomes for Americans and increase upward mobility. What is needed is to revamp that system because it is clearly not working. Instead of welfare programs that encourage people not to work, these programs should allow those who can't work to be able to work. The program should also help those who can't help themselves, but it cannot promote the idea that people who can work do not have to work. Instead, welfare programs should find ways to help people who can't work find work. What is more important is the government should put emphasis on programs that create jobs. This is an important topic of discussion because the US spends a trillion dollars on welfare.

Conservatives and progressives might have different views on how to get people out of poverty, but one thing is for sure: The government has an obligation to find ways to help those who, through bad luck or unfortunate circumstances, cannot help themselves. The main disagreements are around how the government helps the poor. While one side believes that it's the government's job to protect the poor from poverty, the other side of the argument believes in the government's ability to help people out of poverty, so they do not have to rely on the government in the first place. This is why one side of the argument believes in transferring wealth from those who are well off to those who need money. On the other hand, more opportunity is the answer that conservatives give, when it comes to income inequality. Therefore, one side believes that success is measured by how many people are benefiting from the government, while the other side of the argument believes that success is measured by how low the number of people is that are getting help of the government.

American economic exceptionalism should not be measured by how many people are on food stamps. In fact, the growing number of people on food stamps is a proof of failure, failure on behalf of the government to provide programs that allow Americans to work in exchange for getting out of poverty. This not only empowers national and local jobs and keeps Americans jobs in America, it also helps people cover their material needs. Helping people earn their money is helping them earn their success, which is much more fulfilling and dignifying than getting a handout from the government. Government programs can help people find jobs, but they can also help them on the path of entrepreneurship, a path that is highly unlikely for people on welfare. In fact, in many states, it pays better to be welfare than to work a job. In fact, it is more discouraging to work and climb the corporate ladder, thereby earning one's way out of poverty.

There is no denying that the welfare system has helped countless people who truly cannot work for whatever reason. Some people who want to work cannot find jobs and this is a reality due to ever-changing job market. However, United States government efforts for the poor are mismanaged. Instead of giving free handouts for people who can and should work, it should focus on finding programs that direct them to get the right job in career training, sharpen their skills and assimilate them into jobs where they can dignify their lives and enrich the economy.

The economic reform the new president—and future presidents—will need to work on ought to be a plan that benefits Americans and developing countries alike. Recently, there have been several states that needed federal support because of the lack of funding for first responders, due to the upheaval in the mass riots and arson. There was more tension on the streets than there was tension outside the US borders. While one side believes that we need to cut funding for the police, the real recommendation is to increase funding to have better training for the police and better funding for first responders, because, at the end of the day, those are what Americans need the most.

More funding for counties, and cities and states managed by mayors and governors, will also help them organize and allocate those funds towards infrastructure, or where the funding needs to go. This all starts at the federal level, then moves to the states, and finally to the local level. This is pertinent during the existing threat of COVID 19, as states have tackled the virus differently and found different methods that work over others. Overall, the economic situation is going to change inevitably after the pandemic.

Internationally, China has already moved many steps ahead and the landscape of the global economy will surely change soon. America should devise a plan that will reduce its dependence on China and foreign products. This will likely not end its dependence, as every country is dependent on another, but it will strengthen its own economy and diversify the flow of goods. This all ties in with the need to work on international involvement in science and research. Thanks to funding for the vaccine research from the United States, the Biden administration will achieve its vaccination targets soon.

CHAPTER 2

IMMIGRATION IN THE UNITED STATES

One of the biggest problems facing the United States today is its immigration crisis. The fact cannot be denied that immigration actually helped America to be the exceptional country that it is. "Give me your tired, give me your poor, your huddled masses yearning to breathe free" is engraved in the Statue of Liberty, and shows that America is a nation of immigrants searching for a dream.

The first settlers in North America were immigrants, and almost all Americans come from outside the borders of America. The debate over immigration is not a debate of values anymore, but a debate of politics and ideology. Politicians have made this debate very toxic and created a dichotomy among the voters. The United States welcomes around a million immigrants every year, more than anywhere else in the world. Therefore, one should not find themselves trapped between the two sides of zealots who argue for walk in borders or those that believe America should shut itself off from any immigrants. America should and will allow immigrants; the real question is how to go about doing this in a manner that does not hurt the American sovereignty or Americans.

The issue with American immigration is very different than with other countries. America is a country that is built by immigrants, but other nations recognize other features and characteristics to be accepted as a citizen of their country. As well, the United States is the most sought-after country to be in in the world because of the nation's values and the opportunities it promises. When asked about an elevator pitch for the United States, former US Congressman Nick Lampson said, "The American Dream, a better life with greater opportunity than any other place in the world."[70]

There are many issues today regarding immigration in the United States, mainly the idea that immigration is a path to help people out of poverty. This notion is too simplistic and simply not true. For instance, The World Bank regards anyone who makes less than 5.5 dollars per day as desperately poor.[71] Morbid reality hits when we hear about how many people make less than two dollars per day. Three billion people all over the world are considered as the desperately poor, and they come mainly from Africa, India, and parts of Asia.[72] Latin America alone has a population of 100 million who make less than 2 dollars per day.[73] America takes one million out of the three billion every year, which is still the most of any country. It should be noted that one million immigrants coming into the United States already presents some difficulties, including overwhelming the physical and social infrastructure.

The issues with immigration are not just with America; they are also issues for the countries that part ways with those million immigrants. Usually, the immigrants who come into the United States are those who are better educated, more aware, and desperate to leave. They are also amongst the youngest and most energized. What must be realized is that those three billion impoverished people around the world are not going to go to any rich country. However, lifting people out of poverty is not one dimensional. The only place

---

[70] Sataista, https://www.statista.com/statistics/913999/south-america-income-per-capita
[71] The World Bank, 2018, Nearly Half the World Lives Less than $5.50 a Day, https://www.worldbank.org/en/news/press-release/2018/10/1
[72] Ibid.
[73] Population under $2 a Day: Countries Compared, Natin Master, https://www.nationmaster.com/country-info/stats/Economy/Poverty/Population-under-$2-a-day

the impoverished can succeed and lift themselves out of poverty is where they already live.

The elites and their pathological altruism seem to think that taking a million immigrants per year and putting them in the United States is going to make a dent in world poverty. While these elites are allowing for the million to enter the country, only to barely scrape by, another five million impoverished are born. There is no way America can keep this up at the expense of national security and public safety.

The United States has never had more immigrants in population percentage than it has today, and this ratio has only been this high since 1890. This is partly because of chain migration, which adds around three members of family from the million, making it a potential 3.4 million immigrants every year. Also, America does not regulate who comes into the US. For instance, diversity visa programs allow hundreds of thousands a year, requiring no high school, no technical skill or even allegiance of American values. Instead, it's all about nepotism. If one member of the family comes to the United States through one of these programs, they are allowed to bring in members of their family.

Keep in mind that these numbers refer to people who legally come into the United States. If that's not a problem as of yet, then illegal aliens surely will be. While the number of illegal immigrants is around 11 million, it seems that the actual number is much higher and growing by the month.[74] Also, children of illegal immigrants who could be American born citizens are entitled to education, health care and welfare benefits.

"We The People" have the right and the responsibility to control who and how many come into this country. America remains a nation that was built by immigrants, but if she does not contain the flow and manage the loose border, then she will fall prey to her own

---

[74] Raven Clabough, 2018, Number of Illegal Immigrants in U.S. Much Higher Than Previous Estimates, New America.

compassionate nature to help others in the world. However, this view has been demonized and given the cliché "racist" badge. In reality, it is not hateful or racist to want to protect US borders or values. In fact, if Americans do not protect their sovereignty, then the dreams of the many who want to come here will also be destroyed.

While immigration should remain a possible path, America should strengthen its borders to gain better control. This will also help the United States with more effective solutions against the drug epidemic and defend against possible international terrorism. Furthermore, it will help unemployed citizens to find jobs easier, especially those who are in need.

However, it would be hard pressed to say that any walls or barriers are going to prevent people from coming into the United States. As strong and as complicated as the systems we use to prevent people are, illegal immigrants are also finding innovative ways that can bypass those systems, and those ways might be more dangerous. Therefore, it's important to control and expand legal pathways available to migrants and asylum seekers from the Northern Triangle region. This won't be made possible without the help of countries that have the migrants in order to establish a system that is beneficial for legal pathways and migration.

CHAPTER 3

FOREIGN POLICY AND THE UNITED STATES IN THE FUTURE

Foreign policy and diplomacy have been either a hit or a miss, and in the past two decades it has mostly been misses. The United States is still viewed as the world's policeman. It spends billions on its military that goes abroad and fights for the causes of other nations, while other countries stand and watch. America has been keeping this promise since the Second World War, even after the fall of the Soviet Union. America should not be the world's policeman, and it should not waste resources on fighting for other nations. Instead, America should focus its efforts on making peace.

Wars in the future do not seem to be fought with weapons and ammunition, but with innovation and expansion. The world has existed for thousands of years by the physical strength often called "the law of the jungle". When it comes to wars, it is the size of armies and the power and strategies of the armies that matter for international influence. However, wars and physical conflict between countries will one day cease to exist and people are aware of that. While the air is still tense between China, Russia and the United States, any war would be a huge disadvantage to all parties, and America in particular has signed treaties that prevent countries from going to war. Additionally, this is no way shape or form an invitation to have all countries eliminate borders; in fact, it's quite the opposite. Borders should be strengthened, but military involvement around the world ought to end. However, the involvement of the United States should not be forgotten. As the world's largest military, the US needs to secure peace relations as needed. Moreover, working on ways to establish tranquility, economic freedom, and technological advancement is far superior to wasting precious American lives and tax-payer dollars on meaningless wars. Wars will likely exist, but instead of the fighting with ammunition, wars will be fought with brains, technological advancements, and economic expansion.

America does not seek to be the mightiest and scariest nation in the world, nor should it. The foreign policy of the United States is to achieve happiness and help the rest of the world do the same. Therefore, for the prosperity of foreign policy concerning the United States, these steps ought to be followed to a certain extent.

First, the United States should absolutely lead the way when it comes to technological advancements in areas such as transport, energy, artificial intelligence, data science and biotech. As well, the United States should cement its position as the world leader of academia and science. However, this should not be exclusive to American territory, but should expand further to helping other nations do the same.

Second, the United States should lead the way, but not be alone, in diffusing tensions in the Middle East. The big powers of Saudi Arabia, Turkey and Iran having been in a war zone since the First World War, and the needless suffering remains. While the United States military is there for a short time to defend people, it will never be there forever. Therefore, reconciliation has to be made with the neighboring countries to a certain extent and the same would be made with countries such as Syria. Just like nations in the line of Morocco and the United Arab Emirate have put aside their ideological religious sects to side for a peaceful and hopeful future free of conflict, the other countries should do the same. This will not only ensure the stability of certain countries, it will also keep other countries from meddling, such as Russia, Iran, and possibly China, which is what NATO wants as well. The UN, along with America, should find a satisfactory solution for mutual security.

Third, the United States should adopt a more case-based foreign policy with minimal involvement in international conflict. Americans should ask themselves questions that concern their security and the security of their allies. It's also important to decide when it is appropriate to use force for diplomacy. As well, it is appropriate for Americans to ask themselves about the missions and the goals of any endeavors the US is engaged in outside of home turf. Is it national security? Security of our allies? Or could it be the spread of American values.

In the case of the mission in Syria, the goal was to prevent the resurgence of ISIS but the goal is less likely to be achieved. Syria has become the debris of a devastated country, with ravaged infrastructure and hundreds of thousands of people leaving their homes and becoming migrants. Is this a real achievement on which the US can take pride?

Iraq was invaded based on the wrong information for which US had to confess later on, but until then, the country had been devastated.

America's role has never been effective and justified in addressing the issue of Palestine. The US came back from Iraq, but danger is still there and it is always going to remain. However, Americans have to ask themselves questions concerning the cost benefit of these operations. These are questions that must be answered, not only for the case of Iraq, Afghanistan and Syria, but also for US troops in South Korea, Japan, Germany and the ties to NATO. After twenty years, the US finally realized it should pull out from Afghanistan. What was the result of Afghanistan and Vietnam Wars? Thousands of American soldiers were killed and the budget that was supposed to be spent on the well-being of American people was wasted on fruitless and directionless wars.

Climate change has been a topic of foreign affairs more than it has been a topic of environmentalism. That is why the United States again joined Paris Climate Accord—to end public financial support for fossil fuels, reallocating these funds for low-carbon infrastructure and skills development across the country for a transition to a cleaner and more dynamic economy, based on more renewable energy. America has always set the standards for the greater cause and climate change is no different. This is also going to create countless opportunities for clean energy sector workers, and will prove to be an excellent strategy for the long term.

CHAPTER 4

THE CHANGING SOCIAL STRUCTURE

America has struggled with its social structure in recent years, more specifically, in the family. The family is the building block of civilization and statistics show that married couples with children have better finances, better education, better mobility, and their children have higher academic achievements and a better future.

However, in recent years, policies have penalized marriage. For instance, the marriage penalty is one way that discourages couples from getting married as it increases the taxes. In addition, welfare programs have consistently enabled single mother households, rather than helping families. As well, both men and women feel discouraged when it comes to marriage. Men feel the weight of the dangers of divorce as it provides a threat to their finances, and women often have it better if they get divorced since the government provides them with economic stability. Nevertheless, children of single mothers are more likely to drop out of school, commit crimes, or develop mental illnesses. The government and social institutions need to look at the building block of America, which is the family; it's how parents can instill the values that make America great.

More broadly, America faces a bigger threat of a great divide within its nation. This divide is based on color, race, ethnicity and political ideology. Though this divide in the past has provided for more diversity, today's current divide is nothing short of toxic. Most Americans agree that the political realm has made it worse for social unity, as one half of Americans believe in freedom of speech, while the other half shames and cancels anything that does not add up or fit the narrative they want to maintain.

The debate of conservatism and progressivism has divided more Americans than ever. Americans today identify with their ideology more than they identify with American values, and this creates a bigger and bigger social divide. In fact, renowned author, Ondi Laure, believes that one of the barriers to exceptionalism in today's world is this very divide:

> Moving into 2021, The United States of America has the opportunity to regain the mantle of "American Exceptionalism" on the world stage only if we as a nation are willing and able to reclaim the unity that was once part of our American culture. Today, America is far too divided to hold such a title.[75]

Laure also believes that a part of what made the United States great is its acceptance of diversity—diversity of races and religion under one flag and a set of values. However, if those set values are tampered with, then the real divide is a divide over America itself. She explains:

> My elevator pitch of American Exceptionalism is this consistent acceptance of diversity where all differences are what makes America unique. America is the one country where diversity is celebrated" she adds that her one of the unique traits that America is known is the acceptance of diversity "American Exceptionalism" is characterized in united diversity and acceptance...[76]

---

[75] Comment by Ondi Laure recorded in reply to a question, 2021.
[76] Ibid.

Diversity of opinion is fine by all means, but what should not be agreed on is one side having hegemony over opinion. Conservative views have been canceled, as tech companies hold the monopoly over opinions. Free speech is under attack. Many have also lost their jobs because of their views on social media that merely express their opinion on certain matters. It is a general perception that racism is on the rise and white supremacy is being ensured at every level. This is certainly not the America that its Founding Fathers have yearned for. This is a sentiment shared by many Americans, including the likes of Former US Ambassador Sada Cumber. He mentioned that the peak for American social life was in the 1980s and we have moved far from it: "we have moved away from that creed and now stand divided and polarized ...."[77]

Politics have been infused into every issue in America, including health care, policing, foreign policy and even freedom of speech. In recent years, identifying with a certain party has either made you a lunatic extremist or a best friend. This is an unhealthy way of living with each other in a country that prioritized the rule of the people over parties or governments. Politicians know this and use it to their advantage. In fact, Former US Congressman Nick Lampson stated the following when asked about if the United States holds the mantle for American Exceptionalism:

> Yes. The thought of American Exceptionalism still exists. However, recent actions by our leadership have seriously undermined people's impression of what America is. It can return when we get our act together and if it is done in a quick time period.[78]

---

[77] Comment by former Ambassador Sada Cumber recorded in reply to a question.
[78] Comment by former Congressman Nick Lampson recorded in reply to a question.

However, the real divide has also been the mainstream media that has been fueling the hate between Americans. These mega corporations no longer care about being credible or providing citizens with information about what is actually happening; what they care about is outrage culture and what clip is going to attract the greatest number of views, clicks and revenue, and what party is going to enjoy that take. In short, this is propaganda broadcasted into smartphones and TVs, and while history used to be told by the winners, information is now bought and sold in an ideological political auction.

This has created more division, which is clearly seen in today's politics. It can be exemplified in the great exodus from California, with countless people either going to states such as Texas, Arizona, and Nevada due to California's highest state taxes, absurd housing prices, and pathetic management of cities, counties and the state in general, which goes back to the idea of mismanagement of funding.

Next is a brief look into the American health care system.

Regardless of what beliefs you identify with, it's clear as day that the United States health care system is in dire need of an overhaul. While Medicare and Medicaid were created with good intentions, they inevitably caused the prices for health care to skyrocket and caused choices to drop. Newer policies by Obama caused premiums to increase for insurance. Choices have also gone down, while the price of premiums has doubled between 2013 and 2017.[79]

Americans have less choices when it comes to their health care options and doctors. This draws the question: How best to approach about health care? One option is to let the consumers choose what they want. Letting consumers choose what health plan they need according to their condition allows for competing markets, innovation and lower costs. The other option is standardizing health care by the

---

[79] Edmund Haishmaier & Doug Badger, 2018, How Obamacare Raised Premium, The Heritage Foundation, https://www.heritage.org/health-care-reform/report/how-obamacare-raised-premiums

government and letting it run the show. This might prove to be more democratic, but it is not individualistic. Different people need different levels of healthcare, and Americans want to be given the choice. Opponents to this choice feel that this is where the government should come in to protect those who need health care, but cannot afford it, while allowing people who can afford to get better health care, to do exactly that. This is obviously going to take a lot of time, but small steps in the right direction will eventually lead to the goal of a better health care system .

These are steps and plans for the Biden administration to think about and manage. The social divide due to the political dichotomy needs to be fixed as soon as possible. America needs leadership from his office in order to satisfy the needs of all Americans, be they Republican or Democrat. What is more important is that as a president, his office's efforts need to focus on instilling American values before embracing party ideologically.

When it comes to the way that the virus is being handled as of late, the most important thing will be technology and continued vaccine research and distribution. America is also the leader when it comes to vaccine variation, and it is likely that the virus will not simply die off. As many health professionals have pointed out, Americans will simply live with the new virus just like the flu. However, as America gains immunity from the vaccine, mankind's immune system will be better equipped to fight it off. As America has now developed the vaccine, the pharmaceutical companies are now sending vaccines to other nations and collaborating on its distribution. This will not only help low-income countries in reentering the WHO financial aid, but it will also provide another opportunity for America to be a leader of the world.

PART FOUR

CONCLUSION
IS AMERICA EXCEPTIONAL, OR IS
IT A NATION IMPRISONED IN MYTHS?

While writing these lines, I am reminded of those myths, phrases and notions that have been used as rhetoric by presidents, policy makers, political scientists and critics. According to these myths, America is an exceptional and unique country that has a certain mission, and has been destined and prophesized to be the leader of the free world. Since America is "God's country," God is on its side in each venture. The unique values of individual liberty, democracy, freedom, and equality make America exceptional in the world and it has an ordained responsibility to lead the world and liberate other nations from oppression and tyranny. On the surface, these phrases and myths fascinate us and lend force and appeal to the oratory of the politicians; as a matter of fact, America as a nation seems to be imprisoned in this rhetorical expression. Instead, Americans have become victim of these myths and fall complacent by these very flowery slogans.

On June 24, 2012, the TV series "Newsroom" premiered in the United States on HBO. It was watched by 2.1 million viewers, making it one of HBO's most-watched series premiered since 2008. In the miniseries, there is a scene that has now been watched by roughly 1 million viewers on YouTube. This scene shows three candidates being interviewed on a college campus, and all three of the candidates are asked the question, "In one sentence or less, what is it that make America Exceptional?"

The liberal candidate was very quick to respond by saying "diversity and opportunity." The conservative candidate had his canned response ready of "freedom and freedom, so let's keep it that way." Then they came to the character played by Jeff Daniels, and after attempting to provide non-answer platitudes, he launched into the following diatribe:

> It's not the greatest country in the world, professor, that's my answer.
>
> And [to the conservative panelist] with a straight face, you're going to tell students that America's so star spangled awesome that we're the only ones in the world who have freedom? Canada has freedom, Japan has freedom, the UK, France, Italy, Germany, Spain, Australia, Belgium has freedom. Two hundred seven sovereign states in the world, like 180 of them have freedom.
>
> And you—sorority girl—yeah—just in case you accidentally wander into a voting booth one day, there are some things you should know, and one of them is that there is absolutely no evidence to support the statement that we're the greatest country in the world. We're seventh in literacy, twenty-seventh in math, twenty-second in science, forty-ninth in life expectancy, 178th in infant mortality, third in median household income, number four in labor force, and number four in exports. We lead the world in only three categories: number of incarcerated citizens per capita, number of adults who believe angels are real, and defense spending, where we spend more than the next twenty-six countries combined, twenty-five of whom are allies.

None of this is the fault of a 20-year-old college student, but you, nonetheless, are without a doubt, a member of the WORST GENERATION EVER. So when you ask what makes us the greatest country in the world, I don't know what you're talking about?! Yosemite?!!!

We sure used to be. We stood up for what was right! We fought for moral reasons, we passed and struck down laws for moral reasons. We waged wars on poverty, not poor people. We sacrificed, we cared about our neighbors, we put our money where our mouths were, and we never beat our chest. We built great big things, made ungodly technological advances, explored the universe, cured diseases, and cultivated the world's greatest artists and the world's greatest economy. We reached for the stars, and we acted like men. We aspired to intelligence; we didn't belittle it; it didn't make us feel inferior. We didn't identify ourselves by who we voted for in the last election, and we didn't scare so easy. And we were able to be all these things and do all these things because we were informed. By great men, men who were revered. The first step in solving any problem is recognizing there is one—America is not the greatest country in the world anymore.[80]

Although the statistics and factual data that Daniels recounted were from the 2012 timeframe, many of these same relative numbers and statistical data exist today. Before any country can go down the path of a self-affirming title of exceptionalism, it must first breakdown its own strengths and weaknesses, and better understand its own future trajectory. In short, that country must remind itself that "the first step

---

[80] Glinnis Macnicol, 2012, The unreal dystopia of Aaron Sorkin, https://www.politico.com/states/new-york/albany/story/2012/06/the-unreal-dystopia-of-aaron-sorkin-067223

in solving any problem is recognizing there is one. America is not the greatest country in the world anymore."[81]

This book, and the intended outcome, is designed to continue the analysis and discussion about what problems exists in America today, and what are the best solutions to these problems.

AMERICA, THE POLICEMAN'S ROLE

Feeling proud on great values sounds good, but using these as a vehicle and excuse to play a policeman's role for other countries is different thing. Any countryman would push forth their nationalistic view that praises their nation. Any nation in that sense has a certain feeling of pride, but no one does it better than America. History provides abundant examples that before starting every war, this mantra was repeated. All wars, including Cold War, Korea War, Vietnam War, War on Terror, Iraq War, Libya War, Syria War, and other indirect wars were started with the sentence that we, as a nation, have an ordained responsibility to liberate the world, introduce democracy, save children and eliminate extremism and terrorism from the world.

Renowned social scientist, Stephan M. Walt, in his article published in Foreign Policy magazine discussed this concept in these words:

> This unchallenged faith in American Exceptionalism makes it harder for Americans to understand why others are less enthusiastic about U.S. dominance, often alarmed by U.S. policies, and frequently irritated by what they see as U.S. hypocrisy, whether the subject is possession of nuclear weapons, conformity with international law, or America's tendency to condemn the conduct of others while ignoring its own failings.

---

[81] Stephan M. Malt, Nov 2011, The Myth of American Exceptionalism, Foreign Policy, https://foreignpolicy.com/2011/10/11/the-myth-of-american-exceptionalism

Ironically, U.S. foreign policy would probably be more effective if Americans were less convinced of their own unique virtues and less eager to proclaim them."[82]

I will quote the words of President Obama when he sent troops to Syria to combat ISIS and terrorism:

America, our endless blessings bestow an enduring burden. But as Americans, we welcome our responsibility to lead. From Europe to Asia – from the far reaches of Africa to war-torn capitals of the Middle East – we stand for freedom, for justice, for dignity. These are values that have guided our nation since its founding. Tonight, I ask for your support in carrying that leadership forward. I do so as a Commander-in-Chief who could not be prouder of our men and women in uniform – pilots who bravely fly in the face of danger above the Middle East, and service-members who support our partners on the ground.[83]

It is argued that as a nation, Americans have become hostage to this myth and pride. What looks more plausible is that the unholy alliance between politicians, big corporations, business groups and military-industrial complex have continued to hammer these slogans and myths upon the minds of Americans, and fulfilled their hidden agenda by serving the interests of the power club of the country. Each side of the equation uses this phrase differently to get what they want out of it, and each interprets it differently. This did not allow Americans to think out of the box, and they believed in what the power brokers said, which resulted in the weakening of democracy, rule of law and constitutionalism, concentration of wealth in the hands of some groups and widening the gap between rich and poor. To achieve

---

[82] Walt, Stephen M. *The Myths of American Exceptionalism, Foreign Policy*, November 2011.
[83] CNN, Transcript: President Obama's Speech on Combating ISIS and Terrorism, September 10, 2014.

their immediate gains, these forces created division in the society and promoted hate among the communities.

So, I must ask the question: Should America continue to provide the global police force for the world?

AMERICA – THE LAND OF LIBERTY AND EQUALITY

The American nation that was justified in taking pride on the values of equality and individual liberty is no longer seen as an exceptional nation. Indeed, the values of equality and liberty are in great danger. Even after more than two hundred fifty years, America has not eliminated discrimination based on color, language, religion and ethnicity. Americans ought to let go of the idea that they are supposed to do more than other nations.

At a time when other nations have been down due to the Second World War, it was a good initiative by America to pick them back up again, and help establish their economies, but neither USA nor any other nation should police other countries. Sean Adl-Tabatabai, a political commentator, wrote in his article published in News Punch that America is being governed by some invisible government:

> Over the last 214 years, past presidents and political leaders have tried to warn the public that the U.S. government is under the control of an "invisible government owing no allegiance and acknowledging no responsibility to the people.[84]

In the article he further wrote and quoted:

> They virtually run the United States government for their own selfish purposes. They practically control both parties... It operates under cover of a self-created screen [and] seizes

---

[84] Adl-Tabatabai Sean, *Six Former US Presidents Warn About 'Invisible' Shadow Government*, News Punch, January 3, 2016.

our executive officers, legislative bodies, schools, courts, newspapers and every agency created for the public protection.[85]

So, if both political parties run the US government for their own selfish purposes, I must ask, "Is there truly a sense of liberty and equality in America? Or are these characteristics merely a political manipulation caused by the "invisible shadow government?""

AMERICA – A LAND OF DEMOCRACY, PRINCIPALS OF FREEDOM AND RULE OF LAW

The greatest challenge to this country is for democracy, which today is facing so many crises and dangers. Politicians of either party do not have a strong bond with the people who elect and send them to Congress. We have seen the trend of politicians making promises to the people, then doing the exact opposite too many times. The moment individuals reach Congress, Senate, or state legislatures, they start working for special interest groups and divorce themselves from the needs and aspirations of individuals. The government is being run as a corporate entity with a typical business pattern.

It is the responsibility of Americans to remind those in Congress that they are not above the law, and are public servants that "We The People" get to choose and replace according to what we believe as a democratic nation.

Democracy is linked with the rule of the law and constitutional order. The danger associated with democracy also shifts to constitutional order and rule of law. Theodore Roosevelt discussed these fears and challenges in his autobiography, in more robust tone:

Behind the ostensible government sits enthroned an invisible government owing no allegiance and acknowledging no responsibility to the people. To destroy this invisible government,

---

[85] Ibid.

to befoul the unholy alliance between corrupt business and corrupt politics is the first task of the statesmanship of the day.[86]

Following the last election, on a scale of 0 to 100, with 100 being a total democratic breakdown, a survey of independent experts by the Protect Democracy Project scored the current level of threat to America democracy at 56, indicating "substantial erosion," with spikes in "executive constraints," "elections" and "rhetoric."

"We're on a knife's edge ... "the Republic is in serious jeopardy," said Eddie S. Glaude Jr., chair of the department of African American studies at Princeton University.[87] Still, some scholars say that a backsliding democracy is still a democracy that can be protected and fortified, from the bottom up even if not from the top down.

However, I would ask, even though some draw historical parallels to countries that have faced totalitarianism, or have experienced contested elections that became violent—Germany, Kenya, Venezuela, Ukraine, and others—where do you think the American democracy is heading?

THE AMERICAN CONSTITUTIONALISM

The debate of Original Intent and interpreting the constitution has created serious challenges for the smooth functioning of the country. Positivism and Revisionism fueled this discussion in different era of United States history. This debate still goes on. Judicial activism played an important role in providing food for this controversy. However, there is a group of judges who do not give importance to original intent of the Founding Fathers and think that decisions should be made according to the needs and spirit of the current age. By doing so, their decisions are posing threats and challenges to constitutional order.

---

[86] Roosevelt Theodore, *Theodore Roosevelt, An Autobiography*, April 28, 2005, Dodo Press pp xx.

[87] Amy S Rosenberg, October 5, 2020, *Is American democracy at risk? Philly scholars see creeping fascism and historic parallels*, The Philadelphia Enquirer.

The Constitution has clearly distributed powers among three branches of the government, executive, legislature, and judiciary, but the complaint is the judiciary intrudes in the jurisdiction of executive and legislature. The principle of limited government was enshrined in the constitution by the Founding Fathers with clear jurisdiction of state and national governments. However, on the pretext of crises and emergency situations, national government expanded and intruded in the jurisdiction of state government in various eras. During the recent COVID-19 pandemic, states were forced to follow the instructions of national government.

Polarization and division in politics has divided the nation, and neither group wants to listen to the other. In many parts of the country, one can almost feel like they are in a different nation under a different constitution. The great divide is only getting worse, with the glorification of the presidency as a possible fate. We have seen the hysteria over Donald Trump winning the presidency from the left and the attack on the Capitol Hill at the eve of the ratification of new president Joe Biden by the right.

The Electoral College, in which states with less than half the national population can prevail; the Senate, in which California and Wyoming get two votes each; the enumeration of Congress's limited (in theory) powers; the Bill of Rights and other liberties guaranteed in the Constitution; an amendment process that can be stymied by states containing less than 4 percent of the population; and a Supreme Court that can void laws enacted by elected representatives of the people combine to make our democracy rather undemocratic.

Inclusivity and diversity, hallmarks of American society, are in serious threat. The political and electoral process has been corrupted through campaign donations. Politicians provide benefits to those who give donations in their campaigns. This is an obnoxious circle we are living in. Noted political commentator, Drew Christiansen, has termed it a political crisis in a popularized article:

America's culture crisis has become a political crisis because in a winner-take-all society, the guardrails have been removed. In Citizens United v. Federal Election Commission (2010), the Supreme Court voided limits on contributions to political campaigns, equating money with free speech. As a result, corporations and wealthy individuals gained disproportionate influence on political campaigns.[88]

There is a dire need to introduce reforms in political and electoral system. The system of Electoral College for presidential election needs to be revised so that no president can be blamed for election rigging. The mechanism of campaign donations also needs to be reconsidered. "Major reforms are needed to save our democracy" said Stanford Professor Terry Moe, while discussing the current crisis of democracy in his latest book, *Presidents, Populism and the Crisis of Democracy*. "That's the kind of thing this country needs now," Moe added, "We need something big and transformative. If we want to save our democracy, we must focus on building a truly effective government that is capable of dealing with the basic problems of the modern world. If that can't be done, populist anger will continue to surge."[89]

This begs the question, "Will the next 200 years see a radical shift in the interpretation and reading of the Constitution, or will the Founding Fathers' original intent stand the test of time?"

AMERICA'S FALL OF EXCEPTIONALISM IN AFGHANISTAN

It was August 31, 2021. The last US flight departed from Afghanistan at 3:29 p.m. ET carrying the last US troops to America. Political analysts wrote that the American media was showing the pixelated, night vision goggle produced picture of the last soldier. Major General Chris

---

[88] Christensen Drew, *American democracy is in crisis. Do we have what it takes to save it?* America Jesuit Review, December 10, 2020.

[89] Feder Sandra, "A Stanford political scientist's new book makes the case for major governmental reforms to save U.S. democracy," Stanford News, August 10, 2020.

Donahue, commander of the U.S. Army 82nd Airborne Division, XVIII Airborne Corps was "officially" the last service man to leave Afghanistan. General Kenneth F. McKenzie, the head of the U.S. Central Command, was reportedly saying that "Every single U.S. service member is out of Afghanistan, I can say that with absolute certainty." [90]

Some of the American leaders termed the pullout from Afghanistan on the last day of the August 31st deadline as a "historic success," while the Taliban celebrated this event to mark the independence of the country. In fact, the Taliban leadership announced that "foreign occupation in Afghanistan has ended, and now they were free from twenty long years of an imperialist regime."

As I watched all of this unfold, I was reminded of the statements given by George W. Bush and then British Prime Minister Tony Blaire in 2006 saying, "the days of the Taliban are over."[91] But 20 years later, the Taliban still rule the country, while the American forces are out.

Certain members of the media, think tanks, intellectuals, historians, political analysts, and many political leaders are declaring it a defeat of America and a defeat of a superpower. Donald Trump called it a "shameful defeat, a sheer humiliation." He continued by stating that "it is not a withdrawal; it is a surrender."

Yet Joe Biden, in his briefing, said that "Our mission in Afghanistan was never supposed to have been nation building. It was never supposed to be creating a unified, centralized democracy."[92] So, if there was no mission of spreading democracy or institution building, then was this truly a defeat of American Exceptionalism? Many political commentators will place their spin and attempt to

---

[90] Pentagon Press Secretary John F. Kirby and General Kenneth F. McKenzie Jr. Hold a Press Briefing, August 30, 2021.

[91] The White House, August 2006, President Bush Addresses American Legion National convention, Utah.

[92] The White House, August 16, 2021, Remarks by President Biden on Afghanistan, https://www.whitehouse.gov/briefing-room/speeches-remarks/2021/08/16/remarks-by-president-biden-on-afghanistan

correct the history, but there have been countless commentators who have said that American Exceptionalism is now over because of this hasty withdrawal. A withdrawal that left many wondering if the resolve for the American commitment to world peace and our alleys remains. And if it does remain, how will this historic event be viewed on a geopolitical front?

Many say it was a defeat of a big army, but a victory for the Military-Industrial Complex. But all of this begs the question: What are the geopolitical benefits after spending around $3 trillion of US taxpayers' money and fighting a war that has no objective or mission, and how does this affect American Exceptionalism?

Several analysts firmly believe that America has remained in Afghanistan for forty years, and not for the two decades of this last conflict. The first time American forces entered Afghanistan in 1979 was when USSR invaded Afghanistan with a mission to annex and expand communism. America provided significant funds, supplied arms and ammunition, and launched "Jehad" through Afghan Mujahideen with the help of Pakistan. It was a war against the expansion of communism won by Capitalist America. But there is no denying that if Pakistani security establishment and institutions had not helped the USA and Afghan Mujahideen, this war could not have been fought and won. As a result of this war, Pakistan suffered heavy human and economic loss, as more than three million Afghan refugees entered Pakistan and terrorists started heinous activities throughout the country. When Soviet Union was dismembered in 1989, America left the country, abandoned Afghans and Pakistan to cope with the changed circumstances.

Since America did not do anything to improve the Afghan infrastructure, education, health and other civil and political institutions, a civil war started and warlords who were previously fighting against USSR, started fighting against each other by using the weapons of war left by Americans. Different groups of trained Mujahideen fought to get control of the country. Instead of helping Pakistan in this crucial time, America put economic sanctions on Pakistan and pushed it into a difficult situation.

Knowing the fact that Afghanistan is the graveyard of superpowers, America again invaded Afghanistan after 9/11 in 2001. This time the mission was to destroy Al-Qaeda and Osama Bin Ladin. But when these two targets were achieved, the mission statement was changed, and the objective was set to liberate the women of Afghanistan and make the country of Afghanistan a better place to live. After 9/11, just to side with America in its War on Terror, Pakistan had to provide logistic and intelligence support and the Taliban, who were Mujahideen for both America and Pakistan, suddenly became terrorists. Pakistan suffered heavy human and economic losses during this War on Terror. It is said that if, in 1989, Afghans defeated one superpower the Soviet Union, in 2021, they defeated another superpower the United States of America.

Some believe that the defense contractors and the Military-Industrial Complex prolonged this war for 20 years just to amass maximum profits through defense production and supply of weapons. One only needs to spend a few minutes perusing the Department of Defense's military contracts to get a sense of how much money U.S. taxpayers were allotting daily to the war as recently as July 2021. So far in 2021, the Pentagon has awarded $225.83 million in contacts for work exclusively intended for Afghanistan and another $498.08 million for work partly in Afghanistan. Unsurprisingly, these are small sums in comparison to earlier years when military operations were thriving. In just August and September 2015, the DOD contracted $672.95 million solely for what has been terms "America's forever war."[93]

When it comes to foreign policy, American lawmakers seem to be feminists and freedom fighters only when it's convenient. Otherwise, human rights and democracy serve as buzzwords and stratagems, too easily wielded by a military establishment that believes global problems

---

[93] Shaan Sachdev, 2021, The war in Afghanistan was a huge victory—for the military-industrial complex, Salone, https://www.salon.com/2021/08/22/the-war-afghanistan-was-a-huge-victory--for-the--military-industrial-complex

require military solutions, which in return require half of Congress' discretionary spending."[94]

At the end of war in Afghanistan, President Biden gave remarks in a press briefing. "After more than $3 trillion spent in Afghanistan—a cost that researchers at Brown University estimated would be over $300 million a day for 20 years in Afghanistan—for two decades—yes, the American people should hear this: $300 million a day for two decades."[95]

According to the Costs of War Project at Brown University, nearly 20 years after the United States' invasion of Afghanistan, the cost of its global war on terror stands at $8 trillion and 900,000 deaths.[96]

Unfortunately, America seeks military solution to many problems, and exudes a foreign policy of using force. Oftentimes, it uses force first, then diplomacy. It annexes first, then talks about human rights and democracy. After Vietnam, Iraq, and Afghanistan, the American Exceptionalism, which was arguably tasked to spread democracy and freedom and lead the world in pursuance of peace and stability in the world, seems wounded and crying for the urgent care and cure.

Tragically, the idea of American Exceptionalism has been weaponized, thus turning the United States into an empire by default. Iraq and Afghanistan are just the latest examples of this hubris. According to Fawaz A. Gerges, "As the most powerful nation in the world, the United States must resist the temptation to shoot first and ask questions later. This has been a recipe for disaster in Vietnam, Iraq, Afghanistan and beyond. U.S. leaders must rid themselves of a

---

[94] Ibid.

[95] The White House, August 16, 2021, Remarks by President Biden on Afghanistan, https://www.whitehouse.gov/briefing-room/speeches-remarks/2021/08/16/remarks-by-president-biden-on-afghanistan

[96] Providence R.1.,2021, Brown University, Costs of the 20-year war on terror: $8 trillion and 900,000 deaths, https://www.brown.edu/news/2021-09-01/costsofwar

crusading impulse and a moral superiority complex in international affairs that has done more harm than good to the nation."[97]

What America suffered in terms of human lives, body losses and mental disorders, the statistics given by Katrina Manson are depressing and eye-opener:

> But the US experience tells a harsher story. So far, the undertaking has cost it an estimated $2 Trillion and 2,448 lives. More than 20,700 Americans have been wounded, with hundreds losing limbs. Research suggests that about a fifth of the 775,000 US troops who have served in Afghanistan, some on more than five tours, suffer from depression and post-traumatic stress disorder. More than 45,000 veterans or service members have died by suicide since 2013. Most US veterans now say the wars in Iraq and Afghanistan were not worth fighting.[98]

AMERICA – A COUNTRY IN NEED OF STATESMAN

It can be argued that USA needs statesmen, not politicians. A states-man can see beyond immediate concerns and possesses the abil-ity to lead a nation. A politician follows the immediate and popular demands, and only pays heed to those things that may help them in winning the elections. On the other hand, a statesman thinks about the future generation.

Brian Danoff enumerated the qualities of statesman in his book, *Alexis de Tocqueville and the Art of Democratic Statesmanship*:

---

[97] Fawaz A. Gerges, 2021, The U.S. squandered the world's sympathy by invading Afghanistan and Iraq. What will it learn from defeat?, The Washington Post.
[98] Katrina Manson, 2021, After 20 years in Afghanistan, the US is re-evaluating the exceptionalism that drives its foreign policy, Financial Times.

The task of the democratic statesman is to defend goods higher than mere comfort. To do so he must defend particular institutions, namely religion, the family and local government, that limit desire for material goods while pointing citizens toward superior goods. Both de Tocqueville and Cather suggest that given certain assumptions built into democratic life, this task will prove difficult.[99]

There is a need to instill moral values and principles in the politicians and leadership. A statesman needs to be God-fearing and virtuous person who rises above partisan politics and works for the goodness of people and the nation. This is what the Founding Fathers wanted to have in the character of politicians. A statesman should be a person who stands for the truth and righteousness in the government and thinks himself and the government accountable to God.

Can a system be devised to produce such statesmen? George Washington once said:

> The nation which indulges toward another with a habitual hatred or a habitual fondness, is in some degree, a slave. It is a slave to its animosity or to its affection, either of which is sufficient to lead it astray from its duty and its interest." It is my belief that America needs to recreate and unite these Statesman … community servants if you will … that will take a long-term view of our country, and not merely politicians in search of the next "vote getting scheme.[100]

---

[99] Danoff, Brian and Herbert L. Joseph, Jr., *Alexis de Tocqueville and the Art of Democratic Statesmanship*, Lexington Books, Lanham, MD., 2011.
[100] Transcript of President George Washington's Farewell Address (1796), the Alvin Project at Yale Law School, https://www.ourdocuments.gov/doc.php?flash=false&doc=15&page=transcript

As Washington insinuated, we need more statesman to understand their duty and interest in the truth and righteousness of government, and not to be a slave to animosity or affection of a mere political party. That is my hope … that is my desire … that is my prayer for the future of this great country. I want this country to be exceptional; but exceptional in taking pride in racial equality, justice, equality, freedom, diversity, pluralism, and unity. I want to see this country a leader; but a leader in bringing about peace in the world, a leader in fighting against hunger, famine, diseases, and poverty, a leader in liberating the oppressed nations from oppressors, a leader in helping subjugated people win their rightful struggle of independence and a leader in supporting ideals of democracy and liberty.

AUTHOR BIO

Mr. Ghazanfar Hashmi is a highly decorated expert and PhD Scholar in Public Policy. With multiple degrees from universities in Pakistan and USA and as a celebrated writer, Mr. Hashmi is a multi-lingual savant, with expertise in Public Policy, Public Diplomacy, Literature, and Mass Communication, to name a few. His work in promoting cultural and public diplomacy through engagement with renowned think tanks and research organizations, is being recognized across USA. Given his nearly three decades and expertise in international studies, geopolitical affairs, public policy, and diplomacy, combined with his cerebral knowledge of past civilizations, Mr. Hashmi has spent most of his career pondering and researching the required steps for a nation's exceptionalism.

Early in his career, Mr. Ghazanfar Hashmi held various positions in public and private sector including mainstream media as a director, advisor, anchor person, and head of department for various high-level projects. Consequently, he is well suited to conduct the required research for this book.

However, Mr. Hashmi quickly learned that creating a roadmap or blueprint to exceptionalism is no easy task. So, with continued research, combined with countless debates and conversations, Mr. Hashmi set out to determine, "What exactly, does it mean to be exceptional?" After all, can't you develop metrics, characteristics, or even Key Performance Indicators (KPIs) to judge a country's worth or standing?

How do you know when it is achieved, and more importantly, how do you know when it is lost? What are the character traits and how do you even gauge when a country is exceptional?

Mr. Ghazanfar Hashmi answers these questions and others through his combined knowledge, skills and experience within the pages of this book.

www.ingramcontent.com/pod-product-compliance
Lightning Source LLC
Chambersburg PA
CBHW070113030426
42335CB00016B/2134